Student Activity Workbook

PRENTICE HALL
Glenview, Illinois • Needham, Massachusetts • Upper Saddle River, New Jersey

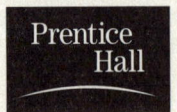

Copyright © 2001 by Prentice-Hall, Inc., Upper Saddle River, New Jersey, 07458.
All rights reserved. No part of this book may be reproduced or transmitted
in any form or by any means, electronic or mechanical, including photocopying,
recording, or by any information storage and retrieval system, without permission
in writing from the publisher. Printed in the United States of America.

ISBN 0-13-043343-8

Table of Contents

CHAPTER 1   **MAKING HEALTHY CHOICES**
- Personal Inventory 1
- Practice 2
- Chapter Review 3

CHAPTER 2   **PERSONALITY AND SELF-ESTEEM**
- Personal Inventory 5
- Practice 6
- Chapter Review 7

CHAPTER 3   **MANAGING STRESS**
- Personal Inventory 9
- Practice 10
- Chapter Review 11

CHAPTER 4   **MENTAL DISORDERS AND SUICIDE**
- Personal Inventory 13
- Practice 14
- Chapter Review 15

CHAPTER 5   **YOU AND YOUR FAMILY**
- Personal Inventory 17
- Practice 18
- Chapter Review 19

CHAPTER 6   **BUILDING HEALTHY RELATIONSHIPS**
- Personal Inventory 21
- Practice 22
- Chapter Review 23

CHAPTER 7   **PREVENTING VIOLENCE**
- Personal Inventory 25
- Practice 26
- Chapter Review 27

CHAPTER 8   **REPRODUCTION AND HEREDITY**
- Personal Inventory 29
- Practice 30
- Chapter Review 31

CHAPTER 9   **PREGNANCY AND BIRTH**
- Personal Inventory 33
- Practice 34
- Chapter Review 35

CHAPTER 10   **CHILDHOOD AND ADOLESCENCE**
- Personal Inventory 37
- Practice 38
- Chapter Review 39

© Prentice-Hall, Inc.   Prentice Hall HEALTH: SKILLS FOR WELLNESS

Chapter 11 — ADULTHOOD, AGING, AND DEATH
- Personal Inventory 41
- Practice 42
- Chapter Review 43

Chapter 12 — FOOD AND NUTRITION
- Personal Inventory 45
- Practice 46
- Chapter Review 47

Chapter 13 — MAKING HEALTHY FOOD CHOICES
- Personal Inventory 49
- Practice 50
- Chapter Review 51

Chapter 14 — DIGESTION AND EXCRETION
- Personal Inventory 53
- Practice 54
- Chapter Review 55

Chapter 15 — MOVEMENT AND COORDINATION
- Personal Inventory 57
- Practice 58
- Chapter Review 59

Chapter 16 — CARDIOVASCULAR AND RESPIRATORY HEALTH
- Personal Inventory 61
- Practice 62
- Chapter Review 63

Chapter 17 — EXERCISE, REST, AND RECREATION
- Personal Inventory 65
- Practice 66
- Chapter Review 67

Chapter 18 — PERSONAL CARE
- Personal Inventory 69
- Practice 70
- Chapter Review 71

Chapter 19 — ALCOHOL
- Personal Inventory 73
- Practice 74
- Chapter Review 75

Chapter 20 — TOBACCO
- Personal Inventory 77
- Practice 78
- Chapter Review 79

Chapter 21 — PREVENTING DRUG ABUSE
- Personal Inventory 81
- Practice 82
- Chapter Review 83

Chapter 22 — INFECTIOUS DISEASES
- Personal Inventory 85
- Practice 86
- Chapter Review 87

Chapter 23 — AIDS AND SEXUALLY TRANSMITTED DISEASES
- Personal Inventory 89
- Practice 90
- Chapter Review 91

Chapter 24 — NONINFECTIOUS DISEASES AND DISABILITIES
- Personal Inventory 93
- Practice 94
- Chapter Review 95

Chapter 25 — A HEALTHY ENVIRONMENT
- Personal Inventory 97
- Practice 98
- Chapter Review 99

Chapter 26 — CHOOSING HEALTH CARE
- Personal Inventory 101
- Practice 102
- Chapter Review 103

Chapter 27 — PUBLIC HEALTH
- Personal Inventory 105
- Practice 106
- Chapter Review 107

Chapter 28 — PREVENTING INJURIES
- Personal Inventory 109
- Practice 110
- Chapter Review 111

Chapter 29 — FIRST AID
- Personal Inventory 113
- Practice 114
- Chapter Review 115

Name _____   Date _____   Class _____

Personal Inventory
Personal Health Sale

To take part in this Personal Health Sale, imagine that each item on the list costs $10. You have $100 to spend as you wish on any ten items that you value. Place a check next to the items you would choose to buy.

_____ Several hours of time outdoors every day to do what you wish

_____ Better looks—being more handsome or beautiful

_____ A lifetime guarantee of never being dependent on alcohol or other drugs

_____ Enjoying the responsibility of making your own choices

_____ The chance to become any other person in the world

_____ Talent to play any musical instrument you want

_____ Perfect health for the rest of your life

_____ Being considered a sensational girlfriend/boyfriend

_____ Ability to eat as much as you want and never get fat

_____ Fame and popularity as an entertainer or politician

_____ Skill to be the top athlete in any sport you choose

_____ Recognition as a successful financial wizard

_____ The chance for adventure, such as mountain climbing or flying

_____ Some close friends you can count on and trust

_____ The cure for two presently incurable diseases

_____ The family you have always dreamed of

_____ An invention that would guarantee clean air and water forever

_____ A peaceful, painless death at a ripe old age

_____ Friendships with famous, influential people

_____ A clear conscience at the end of your life

_____ As much time alone as you want

_____ Ability to end hunger and find homes for the homeless

_____ A wealthy partner or spouse

What did you buy that surprised you? _____

Were there things you thought you would buy but did not? What were they, and why didn't you buy them? _____

_____

What other items would you like to have seen on the list? _____

_____

© Prentice-Hall, Inc.   Prentice Hall HEALTH: SKILLS FOR WELLNESS

Name _____ Date _____ Class _____

Practice

1 Charting a Healthier Course

The plan developed by the United States Public Health Service, called *Healthy People 2000,* emphasizes prevention. Prevention is the practice of healthy behaviors that keep a person free of disease and other health problems. You can practice prevention and set goals to eliminate health risks in your life, but you may need to change some of your behaviors.

The diagram below shows the four steps involved in the process of behavior change. Starting at the bottom step, explain what is meant by the title of each step. Then write one general action a person should take at each step to make his or her behavior healthier.

Steps in Behavior Change for Good Health

Applying Skills

Decision-Making

Knowledge

Awareness

Name _____ Date _____ Class _____

Chapter Review

Key Terms
Use the clues below to identify the words in the puzzle. Write the words on the lines, putting one letter in each blank. When you finish, the word enclosed in the diagonal lines will reveal the concept of health you are aiming for.

1. _ _ _ _ _ _ _ _ _
2. _ _ _ _ _ _
3. _ _ _ _ _ _
4. _ _ _ _ _ _ _ _ _ _
5. _ _ _ _ _ _ _ _
6. _ _ _ _ _ _
7. _ _ _ _ _ _ _ _ _
8. _ _ _ _ _ _ _ _ _ _

1. first step in the process of behavior change
2. the well-being of your body, your mind, and your relationships
3. beliefs most important to you
4. degree of overall satisfaction with your life
5. progression in either direction from one stage to another
6. inherited traits
7. an action that increases the likelihood of a negative outcome
8. physical or mental impairment that limits participation in activities

Define or describe the following terms.

9. social environment _____

10. culture _____

11. prevention _____

12. habit _____

13. Illness-Wellness continuum _____

(Continued)

© Prentice-Hall, Inc.   Prentice Hall HEALTH: SKILLS FOR WELLNESS   3

Name _____

Chapter Review (Continued)

Main Ideas
Answer each of the following questions.

1. How has the meaning of the term *health* changed for most Americans since the beginning of this century? _____
   _____
   _____

2. Why is the current American view of health not relevant to people living in some areas of the world where severe food shortages and violence occur? _____
   _____
   _____

3. What three aspects of well-being are important for your overall health? Describe each.
   _____
   _____
   _____
   _____

4. How can the friends you choose affect your wellness? _____
   _____
   _____

5. How can working in a smoke-filled restaurant after school affect your wellness?
   _____
   _____

6. What types of risk factors besides environmental risk factors can affect your wellness?
   _____
   _____

7. How can regular checkups by a physician help move you toward the wellness end of the Illness-Wellness continuum? _____
   _____
   _____

8. Explain the relationship between behavioral risk factors and the three leading causes of teenage death. _____
   _____
   _____

Name _____ Date _____ Class _____

Personal Inventory
A Healthy Personality

Recognizing one's own personality traits is an important part of having a healthy personality. Read each statement below, decide how it applies to the way you feel about yourself, and put a check in the appropriate column.

Traits	Always	Usually	Sometimes	Seldom/Never
1. I like myself.				
2. I value and trust my own judgment.				
3. I appreciate my own strengths.				
4. I am proud of my accomplishments.				
5. I can accept compliments.				
6. I avoid putting myself down.				
7. I can accept criticism.				
8. I do not feel I have to be perfect.				
9. I can cope effectively with most situations.				
10. I like to set goals for myself and then accomplish them.				
11. I get along well with people.				
12. I have some good friends.				
13. I like meeting different people.				
14. I am aware of my limitations.				
15. I accept things about myself that I cannot change.				
16. I learn from my mistakes.				
17. I am aware of my feelings.				
18. I accept the way I feel about things.				
19. I share my feelings with others.				
20. When I am angry, I express my feelings in an appropriate way.				

Look over your responses. Are there traits you would like to change? Explain why. _____
_____

© Prentice-Hall, Inc. Prentice Hall HEALTH: SKILLS FOR WELLNESS

Name _____ Date _____ Class _____

Practice
Expressing Emotions

Understanding the emotions that you experience and learning to cope with them in positive ways are necessary to your health and well-being.

After reading each of the scenarios below, identify the emotions the main character is probably feeling. Choose from those listed in the box. Give reasons for your answers.

Love	Fear	Happiness
Anger	Guilt	Sadness

1. Lamar was sitting in science class listening to Mrs. Kimball explain a science experiment, when Tonya leaned over and asked him when the chapter test would be. Lamar told her, and Mrs. Kimball heard him. Mrs. Kimball angrily ordered Lamar—and not Tonya—to see her after class.

   _____
   _____
   _____

2. Elena had a bad week. Her boyfriend Hector was badly hurt in an automobile accident. Her father wasn't very sympathetic when Elena told him about Hector.

   _____
   _____
   _____

3. Erika heard today that she made the preliminary cuts for a place on the basketball team. Final tryouts are tomorrow. She can't wait to tell her friend Ann. When she thinks about the tryouts, her stomach begins to hurt and her legs feel weak.

   _____
   _____
   _____

4. Aaron lost his after-school job three weeks ago, and now has no spending money. Two days ago, he saw a new tape he really wanted on his friend Henry's desk. Aaron grabbed the tape and hid it in his own desk.

   _____
   _____
   _____

Choose one of the scenarios above. With a partner, act out how the main character in that scene might cope with the negative emotions that he or she might experience.

Prentice Hall HEALTH: SKILLS FOR WELLNESS

Name _____ Date _____ Class _____

Chapter Review

Key Terms

On the line at the right, write the letter of the word or phrase that best describes each numbered item below. Each word may be used once, more than once, or not at all.

    a. psychologist   **c.** modeling   **e.** rationalization
    b. self-actualization   **d.** extrovert   **f.** psychoanalysis

1. copying the behavior of others   1. _____
2. treatment technique that brings memories into the conscious mind   2. _____
3. person who studies the human mind and behavior   3. _____
4. a friendly and outgoing person   4. _____
5. process by which each person strives to be all that he or she can be   5. _____

Complete the following paragraph using the list of words or phrases below. Each word or phrase may be used once, more than once, or not at all.

    cultural values   modeling   peer group   environment
    heredity   mental health   superego   inborn

Some personality traits, such as friendliness and optimism, are signs of good __(6)__. Most appear to be influenced by a combination of __(7)__ and __(8)__. Inherited traits are biologically passed from parent to offspring and are said to be __(9)__. Through a process called __(10)__, children learn about feelings, attitudes, and appropriate ways of behaving by observing and copying people close to them. Children also learn __(11)__ in this manner. An important influence on the personality of a teenager is his or her __(12)__, or friends.

6. _____
7. _____
8. _____
9. _____
10. _____
11. _____
12. _____

Define or describe the following terms.

13. id _____

14. hierarchy of needs _____

15. self-esteem _____

16. depression _____

(Continued)

Name _____

Chapter Review (Continued)

Main Ideas
Answer each of the following questions.

1. In what way is Freud's theory of personality different from Erikson's? _____
_____
_____
_____
_____
_____
_____

2. Identify and describe three personality traits of a mentally healthy person. _____
_____
_____
_____
_____
_____
_____

3. Compare the defense mechanisms of denial and rationalization. How are they similar? How are they different? _____
_____
_____
_____
_____
_____

Choose the word from the following list that best describes each personality.

aggressive   extrovert   assertive   introvert   passive

4. Sam never tells you what he thinks. He always goes along with the crowd, even though you know he sometimes does not agree.

4. _____

5. Leon is shy about making new friends. He seems to prefer being alone and doing things by himself.

5. _____

6. Jane is annoying and very hard to be around for any length of time. She thinks she is always right and does not mind telling you so.

6. _____

7. Maria is very friendly and outgoing. She makes friends easily and enjoys being with her friends.

7. _____

8. Richard is not afraid to say what he is thinking, and if he disagrees with you, he will tell you so. He also listens to what you have to say.

8. _____

Prentice Hall HEALTH: SKILLS FOR WELLNESS

Name _____ Date _____ Class _____

Personal Inventory
Skills for Managing Stress

Imagine the following potentially stressful situations. How do you usually respond to each of them?

1. When I have too much to do and not enough time to do it,

   I usually _____

2. When I make a big mistake,

   I usually _____

3. When I am very late for something important,

   I usually _____

4. When I am really angry with someone I care about,

   I usually _____

5. When I cannot do something I want to do,

   I usually _____

6. When I lose something that is important to me,

   I usually _____

Look over your responses. What two techniques do you use most often to deal with stress?
_____
_____

How often do you use each of these stress-management skills? Put checks in the appropriate columns.

Stress-Management Skills	Always	Usually	Sometimes	Seldom/Never
Confronting the problem				
Time management				
Physical activity				
Relaxation				
Mental rehearsal				
Biofeedback				
Humor				
Getting help when you need it				

© Prentice-Hall, Inc. Prentice Hall HEALTH: SKILLS FOR WELLNESS

Name _____ Date _____ Class _____

Practice
Signs of Stress

Stress is everywhere in life. To help yourself deal with it, you need to be able to recognize the causes of stress, called stressors. Remember that stress can be positive as well as negative. Often, you can't tell for sure in advance whether a stressor will produce negative stress, called distress, or positive stress, called eustress.

Read the story below. In it you will recognize some stressors. (1) Circle the stressors that are probable sources of distress. (2) Box those that are likely to produce eustress. (3) Underline those that might cause either sort of stress.

Then choose two of the stressors you have underlined. On the lines below the story, describe how each might produce distress or eustress.

> It is 7:30 on a snowy night. Vince, lead guitar player, and the other members of his band are setting up for their first paying job. So far, nothing has gone right. Vince had to spend twenty minutes shoveling his car out of the snow. Kenji could not find his drums. There have been two arguments. Sammy is so nervous that he dropped his keyboard. Then, too, Vince is worried about Maria's playing. She was just accepted to college, and her mind is clearly not on tonight's gig.
>
> Still, because Vince is planning a career in music, he is very excited. At the same time, he's a little scared. "We've practiced hard," he thinks, "but what if I mess up a solo or blow some lyrics?"
>
> This morning, Vince was worried because he just got a new guitar, but now that he sees how good it feels and sounds, he is pleased. He hears the voices of people coming in. Maria gives him a thumbs up. He starts to grin. It's time to go to work.

1. _____

2. _____

10   Prentice Hall HEALTH: SKILLS FOR WELLNESS   © Prentice-Hall, Inc.

Chapter Review

Key Terms

Match each definition on the left with the correct term on the right. Then write the number of each term in the appropriate box below. When you have filled in all the boxes, add up the numbers in each column, row, and two diagonals. The sums should be the same. Some terms may not be used.

A. a person who accepts nothing less than excellence of himself or herself and who often suffers from stress

B. method of managing stress by which you learn to control physical functions

C. an open sore in the lining of the stomach or other part of the digestive tract

D. any situation, event, or person that causes you stress

E. a substance released in your body in response to stress

F. changes that occur during the alarm stage of the stress response that prepare you to react to danger

G. negative stress

H. a personality less likely to develop stress-related symptoms and illnesses

I. the remarkable resistance to stress that some people possess

1. biofeedback
2. distress
3. fight or flight response
4. hardiness
5. adrenaline
6. perfectionist
7. stressor
8. ulcer
9. type B
10. eustress
11. homeostasis
12. type A

(Continued)

Name _____

Chapter Review (Continued)

Main Ideas
Answer each of the following questions.

1. In what important ways is the alarm stage of the stress response different from the exhaustion stage? _____
_____
_____
_____
_____
_____

2. What are two stress-management methods, either positive or negative, that you used to deal with a recent stressor? _____
_____
_____
_____
_____
_____

3. What is the difference between eustress and distress? _____
_____
_____
_____
_____
_____

Label the following situations as sources of eustress or distress.

4. The weather was really bad when you awoke, so you left for school early and arrived on time for band practice.   4. _____

5. Someone close to you has died.   5. _____

6. You got a part in the school play, but rehearsals leave you little time to do homework. Your grades have been dropping.   6. _____

7. Although you felt very nervous at the start of the race, when it was over you discovered that you had broken your previous record.   7. _____

Name _____ Date _____ Class _____

Personal Inventory
Depression and Anxiety

Depression and anxiety are feelings that everybody has at times. Usually, people find ways of working out the problems involved and soon feel better.

How do *you* cope with depression and anxiety? Consider each of the statements below and decide whether or not it applies to you. Write *Always, Often, Sometimes,* or *Never* to describe your usual patterns.

1. Once I get depressed, I cannot seem to get out of it.   1. _____
2. I feel sad more often than I feel happy or content.   2. _____
3. I cannot figure out exactly what is bothering me.   3. _____
4. Things I used to enjoy do not interest me anymore.   4. _____
5. Getting to sleep at night is a problem for me.   5. _____
6. I seldom wake up feeling good.   6. _____
7. I have trouble concentrating on my work.   7. _____
8. I feel tired and worn out most of the time.   8. _____
9. I worry about bad things happening to me, even though I am not sure exactly what they are. 9. _____
10. I have a lot of trouble making up my mind.   10. _____
11. I do not want to be around other people.   11. _____
12. I feel isolated from other people.   12. _____
13. I find it hard to make plans and keep appointments.   13. _____
14. It is difficult for me to express how I feel.   14. _____
15. Other people seem to enjoy life more than I do.   15. _____
16. When I am depressed, I withdraw from others or use other unhealthy coping strategies. 16. _____
17. There are long periods of time when I either lose my appetite or cannot stop eating. 17. _____

Most people will answer *Sometimes* to many of these questions and *Often* or *Always* to only a few of them. If you find that you have answered *Often* or *Always* to most or many of the questions, you may have identified a problem with anxiety or depression.

If you have been experiencing these feelings for a long time—beyond the depression that everyone encounters—you need to do something to help yourself feel better. Your situation may be one that can be helped by reaching out to friends, family, or professional counselors and therapists.

© Prentice-Hall, Inc.   Prentice Hall HEALTH: SKILLS FOR WELLNESS

Name _____ Date _____ Class _____

Practice

The Facts About Suicide

Knowing the facts about suicide may someday help you save someone's life.

With a partner, discuss the warning signs that may be shown by those at risk of suicide and the measures that can be taken to help prevent suicide. Use the format below to help you organize your discussion.

Warning signs that may be shown by those at risk of suicide:

Changes in behavior, such as _____
_____
_____

Changes in personality, such as _____
_____
_____

Comments related to death or suicide, such as _____
_____
_____

Emotional trauma resulting from situations such as _____
_____
_____

Measures that can be taken to help prevent suicide:

Express to the suicidal person that _____
_____

Listen to the suicidal person when he/she _____
_____

Suggest to the suicidal person that _____
_____

Report the suicidal person's condition to _____
_____

Prentice Hall HEALTH: SKILLS FOR WELLNESS © Prentice-Hall, Inc.

Name _____ Date _____ Class _____

Chapter Review

Key Terms

On the line at the right, write the letter of the word or phrase that matches each numbered description below. Each answer may be used once, more than once, or not at all.

- **a.** bulimia
- **b.** case history
- **c.** psychotherapy
- **d.** obsession
- **e.** schizophrenia
- **f.** dementia
- **g.** phobia
- **h.** trauma
- **i.** hypochondria
- **j.** clinical psychologist

1. anxiety related to a specific situation or object 1. _____
2. eating disorder in which individuals go on eating binges followed by purging 2. _____
3. common type of organic disorder characterized by an irreversible loss of brain function 3. _____
4. brief description of an individual who suffers from a particular disorder 4. _____
5. an idea or thought that takes over the mind and cannot be forgotten 5. _____
6. somatoform disorder characterized by a constant fear of disease and preoccupation with one's health 6. _____
7. treatment method that involves conversations with a trained professional who helps an individual overcome a mental disorder 7. _____
8. mental-health professional who specializes in recognizing and treating abnormal behavior 8. _____

On the line at the right, write the word or phrase that best completes each sentence. Each answer may be used once, more than once, or not at all.

cluster suicide mood mental organic
trauma anxiety compulsion dissociative

9. _____ disorders are illnesses that affect the mind. 9. _____
10. _____ disorders have a physical cause. 10. _____
11. A _____ is a painful physical or emotional experience. 11. _____
12. In _____ disorders, a person's fears interfere with normal, everyday functioning. 12. _____
13. A _____ is an unreasonable need to behave in a certain way. 13. _____
14. _____ disorders, such as clinical depression, result when the emotions a person feels become so extreme that they interfere with daily life. 14. _____
15. A _____ occurs when several people in a school or social group attempt to commit suicide. 15. _____
16. In _____ disorders, people become disconnected from their former identities. 16. _____

(Continued)

© Prentice-Hall, Inc.   Prentice Hall HEALTH: SKILLS FOR WELLNESS   15

Name _____

Chapter Review (Continued)

Main Ideas
Answer each of the following questions.

1. Compare psychiatrists and clinical psychologists. How are they alike? How are they different? _____
_____
_____
_____

2. In what ways are anorexia nervosa and bulimia alike and different? _____
_____
_____
_____
_____

3. Identify three theories for the cause of functional mental disorders. Explain each one.
_____
_____
_____
_____

Identify the disorders associated with the following symptoms.

4. Carmela has lost 30 pounds (13 kilograms) in two months and is now seriously underweight. She refuses to eat normally. _____

5. Since his sister's death three months ago, Pierre has had trouble falling asleep. _____

6. Sofia feels panic-stricken whenever she has to get into an elevator. _____

7. After the car crash, a young woman was found wandering the neighborhood. She does not remember her name or anything about herself. _____

8. Akiko got a divorce two years ago and is still so overwhelmed by sadness that she is unable to carry out everyday activities. _____

9. Leon is sometimes so overly excited and talks so rapidly that he is difficult to follow. At other times, he is deeply depressed. _____

10. John always feels anxious and cannot say exactly why. _____

Name _____ Date _____ Class _____

Personal Inventory
Sharing Responsibilities

How do you help out at home? Put a check mark in the column that shows how often you do the task listed at the left. Use the blank lines to enter other ways that you help out at home.

	Always	Sometimes	Never
Every day I			
1. help with the dishes			
2. take out the garbage			
3.			
4.			
5.			
Two or three times a week I			
1. help with the laundry			
2. help with grocery shopping			
3.			
4.			
5.			
On the weekends, I help			
1. prepare meals			
2. run errands			
3.			
4.			
5.			

Why is it important for all family members to help out with the work of running the household? _____
_____

How do you think even small children could help? Why might it be important for a child to have chores? _____
_____

© Prentice-Hall, Inc.   Prentice Hall HEALTH: SKILLS FOR WELLNESS   17

Name _____ Date _____ Class _____

Practice
Family Health

A major factor in determining the wellness of a family is how good its members are at sharing information, thoughts, and feelings with each other—communicating.

Choose one of the following family situations: parents disapprove of teenager's friends, parents frequently fight and mention divorce, sibling constantly borrows teenager's possessions without permission, teenager is depressed about poor grades, siblings disagree about the type of music played in the home, or a family member dies.

Choose two or three of the following family members who might be involved in this situation: mother, father, teenage son, teenage daughter, or sibling.

Choose one or two of the following family-help providers: relative, family friend, clergy, support group member, or family therapist.

Write about the situation. Describe how the people can work together to resolve the conflict, express emotions, and use decision-making techniques to maintain family health.

_____
_____
_____
_____
_____
_____
_____
_____
_____
_____
_____
_____
_____
_____
_____
_____
_____
_____
_____
_____
_____

Chapter Review

Key Terms

On the line at the right, write the letter of the word or phrase that matches each numbered description below. Each answer may be used once, more than once, or not at all.

- **a.** separation
- **b.** single-parent family
- **c.** foster family
- **d.** sexual abuse
- **e.** extended family
- **f.** divorce
- **g.** emotional abuse
- **h.** emotional neglect
- **i.** support group

1. family that provides care and a temporary home for children whose biological parents are unable to care for them 1. _____
2. legal agreement to end a marriage 2. _____
3. arrangement in which spouses live apart and try to work out their problems 3. _____
4. criminal offense in which a child or adolescent is used for sexual purposes 4. _____
5. nonphysical mistreatment of a person 5. _____
6. failure of parents to give their child love and emotional support 6. _____
7. family in which only one parent lives with a child or children 7. _____
8. network of people who help each other cope with a particular problem 8. _____

Complete the following paragraphs using the list of words or phrases below. Each word or phrase may be used once, more than once, or not at all.

nuclear	physical abuse	sexual abuse	support group
relationships	socialization	blended	emotional abuse
Al-Anon	extended family		

Through __(9)__ with family members, a child learns to love, respect, and get along with others. Heads of families have the added responsibility of __(10)__, or teaching children acceptable ways of behaving in society. Families can take many forms. When a mother and a father and their child or children live together, it is a(n) __(11)__ family. This type of family may be part of a(n) __(12)__, a network of close relatives living together or near each other. Many children live in single-parent families. There are also __(13)__ families, with a stepparent, biological parent, and the child or children of one or both parents living together.

Family problems arise from many causes. Alcohol abuse by a family member can be stressful. __(14)__ is an organization that helps people cope with an alcoholic family member. Sometimes family members are victims of __(15)__, which is punishment that leaves a mark that can be seen the next day. Some children or adolescents are subject to unwanted kisses, inappropriate touching, or sexual intercourse, and become victims of __(16)__. Various crisis hotlines can provide help to abused family members. People in a(n) __(17)__ can also help each other cope with a particular problem.

9. _____
10. _____
11. _____
12. _____
13. _____
14. _____
15. _____
16. _____
17. _____

(Continued)

Name _____

Chapter Review (Continued)

Main Ideas
Answer each of the following questions.

1. Why is socialization of children important? _____
   _____
   _____
   _____

2. Your best friend's parents are going through a divorce, and your friend seems very withdrawn lately. How could you help?
   _____
   _____
   _____

3. A husband and wife are both working long hours at their jobs. If neither one likes to cook, how could they handle the household chores of cooking, cleaning, and shopping?
   _____
   _____
   _____

Complete the following chart.

Family Form	Members
Nuclear	
Extended	
Foster	
Single-parent	
Blended	

Prentice Hall HEALTH: SKILLS FOR WELLNESS

Name _____ Date _____ Class _____

Personal Inventory
Checklist for Choosing a Mate

What qualities are really important to you in looking for a partner or mate? Read the list below and make checks by those characteristics that you consider most important.

_____ flexible	_____ sensitive	_____ interesting
_____ creative	_____ sure of own values	_____ responsible
_____ romantic	_____ tolerant	_____ sense of humor
_____ good companion	_____ no hereditary diseases	_____ hard worker
_____ well educated	_____ intelligent	_____ flirtatious
_____ wants children	_____ neat and orderly	_____ fun-loving
_____ expresses feelings	_____ honest	_____ risk taker
_____ good health	_____ loyal	_____ jealous
_____ religious	_____ exciting personality	_____ nonsmoker
_____ from a good family	_____ athletic	_____ careful
_____ kind	_____ sexy	_____ affectionate
_____ aggressive	_____ possessive	_____ friendly
_____ listens well	_____ ambitious	_____ same religion
_____ decisive	_____ physically attractive	_____ avoids drugs/alcohol

From the qualities you checked, choose the four that you think are most important. List them below and explain why you chose them.

First choice: _____
_____

Second choice: _____
_____

Third choice: _____
_____

Fourth choice: _____
_____

Look at the characteristics of a successful marriage in Figure 6-15 on page 136 of your textbook. Which of your four choices most closely match those characteristics? Explain why.

_____
_____
_____

Name _____ Date _____ Class _____

Understanding Friendship

Practice

Friendships are relationships based on trust, acceptance, and shared interests or values.

Fill out the concept map below to organize your understanding about friendships. Then create a cartoon strip that tells a short story about friendship. It must be at least five panels long. You may draw the characters or cut them out from magazines. Write the dialogue between the characters below each panel. The cartoon strip does not need to be funny. Use the concept map to guide your ideas about what you want to show in the cartoon strip.

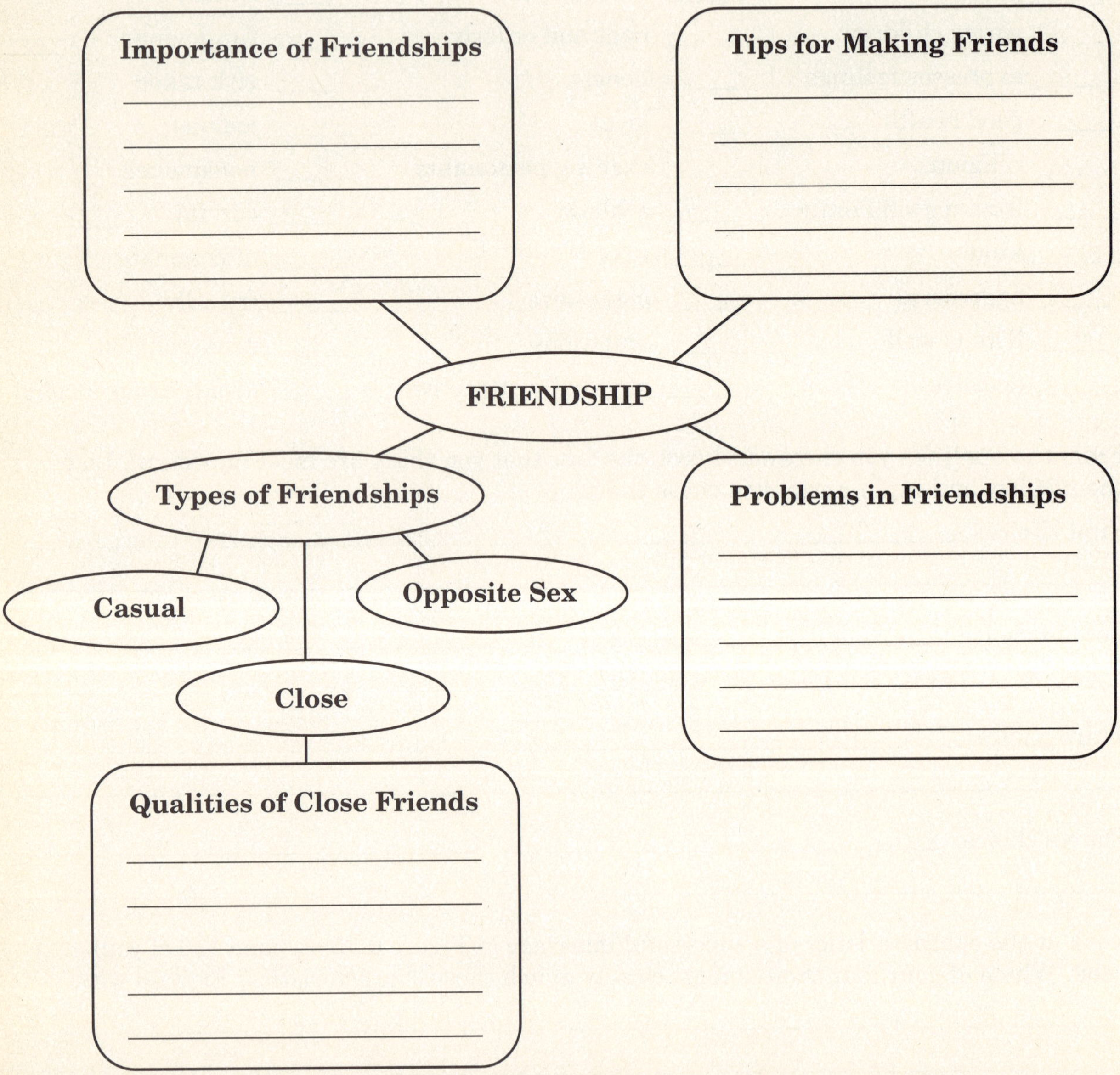

Importance of Friendships
_____
_____
_____
_____

Tips for Making Friends
_____
_____
_____
_____

FRIENDSHIP

Types of Friendships
- Casual
- Opposite Sex
- Close

Problems in Friendships
_____
_____
_____
_____
_____

Qualities of Close Friends
_____
_____
_____
_____

22 PRENTICE HALL HEALTH: SKILLS FOR WELLNESS   © Prentice-Hall, Inc.

Name _____ Date _____ Class _____

Chapter Review

Key Terms
Complete the following paragraphs using the list of words and phrases below. Each word or phrase may be used once, more than once, or not at all.

eye contact   emotional intimacy   passive
compromise   "I" message   body language
empathy   active listening   infatuation
aggressive

Communication, cooperation, and ___(1)___ are three skills that form the basis of a relationship. The kind and quality of a relationship is then determined by the effectiveness of communication. Meeting someone's gaze, or making ___(2)___, is one way to communicate. Another is to express your feelings without judging the other person using a(n) ___(3)___.

Focusing your full attention on the speaker, or ___(4)___, is a good way to make the speaker feel comfortable about expressing personal feelings. You can also communicate nonverbally using ___(5)___ such as gestures and facial expressions.

Often, your opinions and feelings may differ from those of others. Some people are ___(6)___ and hold back their true feelings. Others are ___(7)___ and show their feelings in a threatening way. This type of behavior shows lack of respect for the other person. ___(8)___, a form of give-and-take, is one way to reach an agreement.

During the teenage years, most people experience feelings of intense interest in a particular person. These normal feelings of ___(9)___ help teenagers learn to form strong attachments as adults. Couples capable of ___(10)___ can develop a close relationship that is built on openness, sharing, affection, and trust.

1. _____
2. _____
3. _____
4. _____
5. _____
6. _____
7. _____
8. _____
9. _____
10. _____

Define or describe the following terms.

11. cooperation _____
_____

12. empathy _____
_____

13. clique _____
_____

14. gender roles _____
_____

(Continued)

Name _____

Chapter Review (Continued)

Main Ideas
Answer each of the following questions.

1. What is the difference between assertive communication and aggressive communication? _____
_____
_____
_____

2. Describe what is meant by *body language*. Then explain what is meant by the term *eye contact*, which is an example of body language. _____
_____
_____
_____

3. If you want to know whether people are actively listening, what kind of behavior would you look for? _____
_____
_____
_____

4. What is the relationship between prejudices and stereotypes? _____
_____
_____
_____

Classify the following statements as examples of assertive, passive, or aggressive communication. On the line at the right, write assertive communication, passive communication, *or* aggressive communication.

5. I didn't mind waiting for you. I didn't have anything important to do.

5. _____

6. Why did you wear that coat? It's too dressy.

6. _____

7. I saw you play in the basketball game. You really messed it up for the whole team.

7. _____

8. When I see you flirt with someone, I feel jealous and insecure.

8. _____

9. Why don't we share these chores so we both can leave early?

9. _____

10. We can do whatever you want tonight. I'll catch that movie the next time it's in town.

10. _____

24 Prentice Hall HEALTH: SKILLS FOR WELLNESS © Prentice-Hall, Inc.

Name _____ Date _____ Class _____

Personal Inventory

Your Anger Style Inventory

This exercise will help you determine how you usually deal with anger. Consider each statement below and circle the answer that *most closely* represents how you would probably react.

1. A friend of yours is stealing your girlfriend/boyfriend. You would probably
   a. beat the person up
   b. decide that the person isn't your friend any more
   c. talk with both of them and find out what's going on

2. Some of your friend's opinions make you mad. You would probably
   a. punch him the next time he starts stating his opinions
   b. ignore it—that's what friendship is about
   c. argue with him

3. Some opinions of an acquaintance make you mad. You would probably
   a. hit her
   b. just try to stay away from her
   c. ask her why she feels the way she does

4. When you are angry, which do you do?
   a. Think about throwing something or someone against the wall.
   b. Go for a walk or a run.
   c. Talk things over with a friend.

5. When you're angry, you are likely to
   a. push your friends aside
   b. invite your friends to go with you to a movie or for a walk
   c. tell friends all about your problem

6. It wasn't your fault that you were late getting to school. However, you missed a test and the teacher won't let you make it up. You would probably
   a. think about smashing the windshield of the teacher's car
   b. think, "Okay, so what if I get a failing grade?"
   c. discuss it with the teacher later when you've calmed down

7. When you're in a situation that makes you angry, you often think
   a. No one's going to push *me* around.
   b. All I want to do is get out of here!
   c. I want to clear this up.

8. Lately your boyfriend/girlfriend is nagging you all the time. It's getting on your nerves and making you angry. You would probably decide that
   a. you've had it—next time you'll hit the person
   b. he or she just isn't worth it—you'll break up
   c. this has got to stop—you'll call him or her and talk it out

9. If you started thinking of ways to get even with someone, you would probably
   a. pick the best idea and carry it out
   b. tell a friend your idea, have a good laugh, but leave it at that
   c. decide that it's time to let the person know how you feel

10. You think your friend has let you down in a big way. Next time you see your friend, you would probably
    a. push him or her out of the way and keep walking
    b. pretend nothing has happened
    c. let your friend know you're angry and why

11. A girl you never liked is telling lies about you. You would probably
    a. slap her
    b. ignore it—who cares what she says?
    c. tell her to knock it off or else

12. When you're angry, you often feel like
    a. hitting someone or something
    b. taking a nap
    c. working on the problem until it's no longer a problem

© Prentice-Hall, Inc.   Prentice Hall HEALTH: SKILLS FOR WELLNESS

Name _____ Date _____ Class _____

Practice
How Fights Start

Fights may start for a variety of reasons. Some factors that may lead to fights include arguments, hurt pride or embarrassment, peer pressure, prejudice, revenge, and control.

Each paragraph below describes a situation that may lead to a fight. On the lines provided, identify which factors may influence the characters in the situation to start a fight. Then suggest what might be done to avoid a fight.

A. Sometimes Franklin wishes he were as big as Marcus. Marcus won't admit it, but sometimes he wishes he were as smart as Franklin. Marcus often teases Franklin about being short and being smart in school. This angers Franklin. Franklin feels that he should confront Marcus and tell him off.

_____
_____
_____
_____
_____

B. In the hallway between classes, Dana accuses Teresa of stealing money from her locker. Teresa denies it. Dana's friends gather around Dana, encouraging her to search Teresa's locker for the money. They press Dana forward, coaxing her to fight Teresa.

_____
_____
_____
_____
_____

C. Jake tripped Derek in the hall, causing Derek to drop his books and papers. Derek was hurt and angry. He threatened to get back at Jake.

_____
_____
_____
_____
_____
_____

Prentice Hall HEALTH: SKILLS FOR WELLNESS © Prentice-Hall, Inc.

Name _____ Date _____ Class _____

Chapter Review

Key Terms

Complete the following paragraphs using the words and phrases provided. Each answer may be used once, more than once, or not at all.

victim   free-floating anger   intolerance
assailant   homicide   microinsults
instigators   territorial gangs   discrimination
violence

Acts of ___(1)___, the use of physical force with the intent to injure or kill, are costly to society in many ways. The problem most seriously affects young people from ages 15 to 24, for whom the intentional killing of one person by another, called ___(2)___, is the second leading cause of death. These crimes, however, touch not just the ___(3)___, the person who suffers from the violent act, and that person's ___(4)___, or attacker, but the families of those people and the community around them. Everyone pays a price for violence, whether the cost is physical, emotional, or financial.

The catalysts for violent behavior are varied. Some are found in ___(5)___, arising from the frustration and hostility of people who feel unable to improve their lives. In some families, children learn from their parents to use violence to solve problems. In other situations, highly organized groups of young people, called ___(6)___, use destructive behavior to defend their area's boundaries.

People can learn how to control their anger, despite the pressure of ___(7)___, who encourage other people to fight. People also can be taught how to counteract ___(8)___, or the lack of acceptance of another's beliefs. If people fought the unfair treatment of a person, called ___(9)___, rather than the person, people might be less angry and more understanding toward each other.

1. _____
2. _____
3. _____
4. _____
5. _____
6. _____
7. _____
8. _____
9. _____

Main Ideas

Answer each of the following questions on the lines provided.
1. Discuss why poverty can be a risk factor for violence. _____
_____
_____
_____
_____

(Continued)

Name _____

Chapter Review (Continued)

2. How can children learn nonviolent methods of handling anger? _____
_____
_____
_____
_____
_____
_____

3. Why are territorial gangs called "fighting gangs"? _____
_____
_____
_____
_____
_____
_____

4. What role does control play in violence toward women? _____
_____
_____
_____
_____
_____
_____

5. Under what circumstances should you ignore a conflict? _____
_____
_____
_____
_____
_____
_____

Name _____ Date _____ Class _____

Personal Inventory
Body Image

Just about everyone is dissatisfied with some part of his or her body. Check the columns that describe how you feel about certain parts of your body.

	Body Part	Very Satisfied	OK	Neutral	Could Improve	Dislike
Head and Face	Hair					
	Skin					
	Eyes					
	Nose					
	Mouth/Lips					
	Teeth					
	Chin					
	Ears					
	Neck					
Upper Body	Shoulders					
	Chest/Breasts					
	Arms					
	Hands					
	Fingers/Nails					
	Waistline					
Lower Body	Hips					
	Stomach					
	Buttocks					
	Legs					
	Feet					
Overall	Height					
	Weight					
	Figure/Build					

Review your survey. Do you think you were too critical? Too generous? Are there things you are dissatisfied with that you can change? Which ones? _____

_____

© Prentice-Hall, Inc. Prentice Hall HEALTH: SKILLS FOR WELLNESS

Name _____ Date _____ Class _____

Practice

The Endocrine System

The group of organs known as the endocrine glands releases chemical messengers called hormones directly into your bloodstream. These hormones control your body's development and many of its daily activities.

Working with a partner, write the function of each endocrine hormone on a separate card. Place these function cards face down and mix them well. Draw a card and read the function written on it to your partner. Your partner should respond by telling which hormone and gland match the function, as well as an additional fact about the gland, such as its location in the body. Then reverse the procedure so that your partner draws a card and you respond. Continue until all the function cards have been drawn.

As you play the game, fill in the blanks on the diagrams below with the name of each gland as it is mentioned. Then make a check beside the glands that control the development of the body. Finally, draw arrows from the glands that regulate other endocrine glands to those that they regulate. Use different colored pens or pencils to distinguish each arrow.

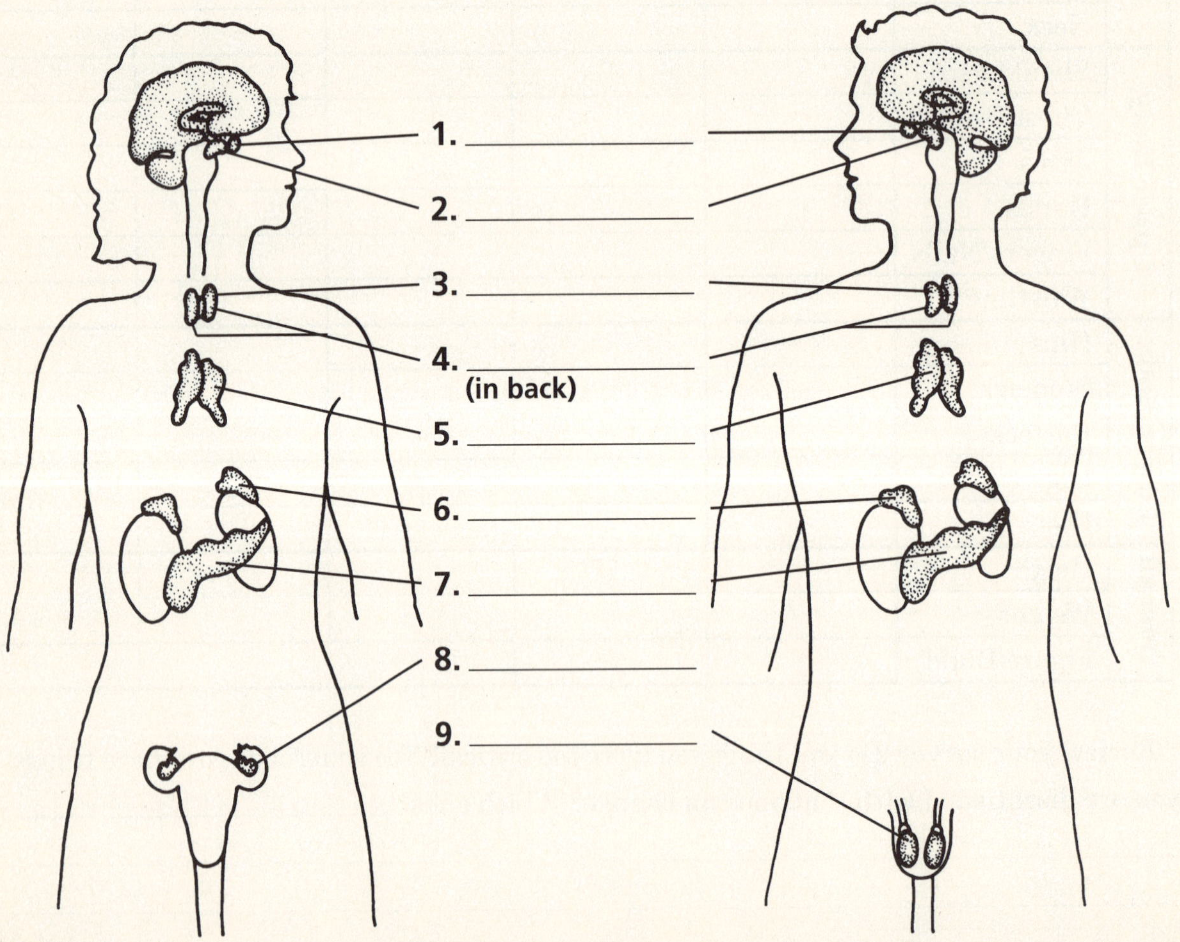

1. _____
2. _____
3. _____
4. _____ (in back)
5. _____
6. _____
7. _____
8. _____
9. _____

30   Prentice Hall HEALTH: SKILLS FOR WELLNESS

Name _____ Date _____ Class _____

Chapter Review

Key Terms

Use the clues to identify the words. Write the words on the lines, putting one letter in each blank. When you finish, the word enclosed in the diagonal lines will tell you the name of the chemical messengers in the body.

1. gland that regulates the rate of metabolism
2. system that controls daily activities and development
3. female sex hormone
4. gland that regulates body temperature and blood pressure
5. male sex hormone
6. discharge of blood and tissue in females
7. substance that increases heart rate, blood pressure, and breathing rate in an emergency

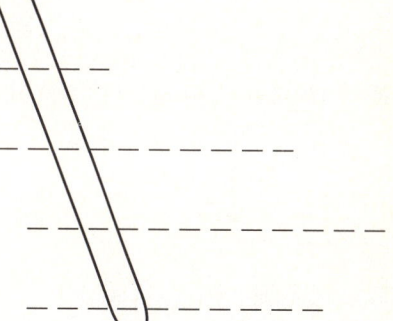

Match each word with its correct definition. Some words may not be used.

- **a.** Down syndrome
- **b.** sex-linked
- **c.** ovaries
- **d.** scrotum
- **e.** menopause
- **f.** PMS
- **g.** thyroxine
- **h.** seminal vesicles
- **i.** luteinizing hormone
- **j.** gene
- **k.** endometrium
- **l.** pancreas

8. thyroid hormone that regulates the body's overall metabolic rate
9. organs that release estrogen and progesterone and produce mature egg cells
10. section of a chromosome that determines a single trait
11. condition marked by nervous tension, mood swings, headache, irritability
12. hormone that affects the testes in males and ovaries in females
13. gland that controls the level of glucose in the bloodstream
14. recessive gene found on the X chromosome

(Continued)

© Prentice-Hall, Inc.   Prentice Hall HEALTH: SKILLS FOR WELLNESS

Chapter Review (Continued)

15. time at which ovaries cease producing mature eggs   15. _____
16. genetic disorder caused by an extra chromosome   16. _____
17. sac containing the testes   17. _____

Main Ideas
Answer each of the following questions.

1. You are walking in the woods when you suddenly see a bear in the distance. Your heart pounds, your breathing quickens, and you feel a lump in your throat. What is happening to your body? _____
_____
_____

2. A routine physical exam shows that the level of sugar, or glucose, in your blood is high. What could cause this? _____
_____
_____

3. Clarence and his wife are unable to have children. A physician has diagnosed Clarence as being sterile. What could account for Clarence's condition? _____
_____
_____

4. Rachel is 48 years old and has had only one menstrual period in the past year. What is happening to her endocrine system? _____
_____
_____

5. How does the sperm cell from the father determine whether a couple's baby will be a boy or a girl? _____
_____
_____

6. Compare sickle-cell disease and hemophilia. How are they similar? How are they different? _____
_____
_____

Name _____ Date _____ Class _____

Personal Inventory

Parenting

Many people have not thought through their feelings about being parents and taking on the responsibilities of parenthood. To explore your own feelings, complete these statements.

1. To me, a family is _____

2. When it comes to planning a family—or just letting things happen—I feel _____

3. The nicest thing about having a baby is _____

4. When a woman is pregnant, she should _____

5. When I think about childbirth _____

6. After a baby is born, the parents' responsibilities are _____

7. The idea of my baby inheriting a disease or defect makes me feel _____

© Prentice-Hall, Inc.   Prentice Hall HEALTH: SKILLS FOR WELLNESS   33

Name _____ Date _____ Class _____

Practice
Birth

Birth is a process that involves various stages and events. Below are described several events that occur during the three stages of labor—events that occur just before, during, and after childbirth. Copy the events onto a piece of paper, cut them out, and arrange them in the order in which they would generally occur.

1. The cervix is dilated to about 4 centimeters.

2. The umbilical cord is clamped and cut.

3. The baby is given an Apgar score.

4. The baby's head is visible.

5. The cervix softens to allow the baby to pass through.

6. The amniotic sac breaks.

7. The placenta is delivered.

8. The uterus begins a series of contractions.

9. Special eyedrops are put in the baby's eyes.

10. The contractions are only a few seconds apart.

11. The baby's mouth and nose are suctioned to make breathing easier.

12. The baby is pushed out through the cervix and vagina.

Name _____ Date _____ Class _____

Chapter Review

Key Terms
Complete the following crossword puzzle.

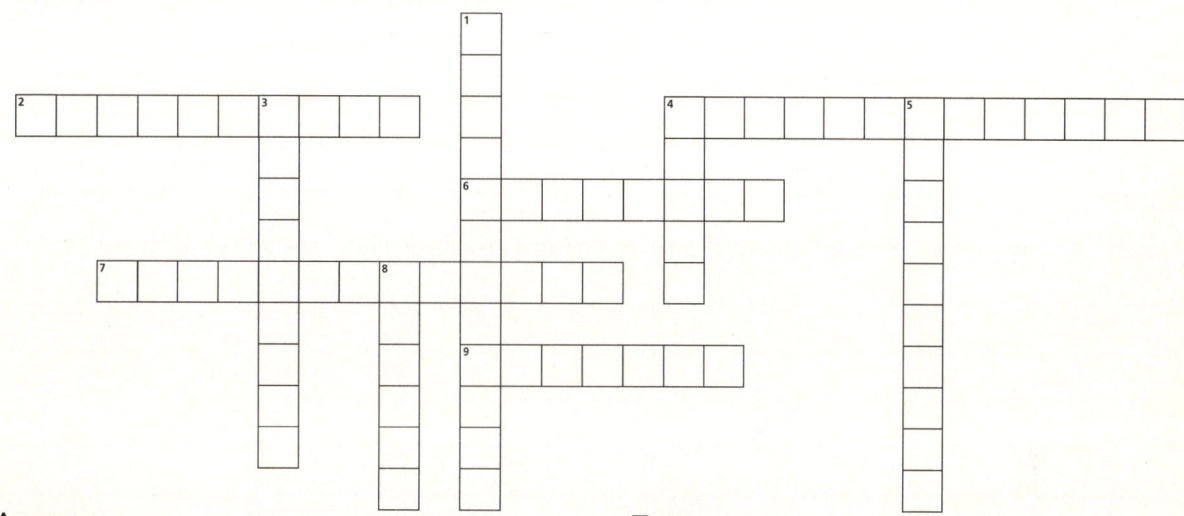

Across

2. delivered in the third stage of birth; another name for the placenta
4. the union of an egg and a sperm
6. fluid that surrounds an embryo
7. preventing pregnancy
9. serious condition characterized by high blood pressure, protein in the urine, and swelling

Down

1. attachment of embryo to wall of uterus
3. unable to produce children
4. unborn baby from two months to birth
5. special chambers for premature babies
8. unborn baby from implantation to two months

Complete the following paragraph using the list of words below. Each word may be used once, more than once, or not at all.

| umbilical | prenatal | delivery | amniocentesis | miscarriage |
| labor | afterbirth | blastocyst | ultrasound | |

A very important part of any pregnancy is the __(10)__ care a woman receives. If a problem is suspected, the obstetrician may recommend __(11)__, the removal of a small amount of fluid from around the fetus. High-frequency sound waves, or __(12)__, can be used to make a "picture" of the fetus. If the pregnancy proceeds with no problems, the mother will go into __(13)__ when the birth process starts. The actual birth of the baby, or the __(14)__, usually lasts from half an hour to two hours. Once the baby is out of the mother's body, the umbilical cord is cut. Labor ends with the delivery of the __(15)__.

10. _____
11. _____
12. _____
13. _____
14. _____
15. _____

(Continued)

Name _____

Chapter Review (Continued)

Main Ideas
Answer each of the following questions.

1. Compare adoption and foster care. How are they alike? How are they different?
   _____
   _____
   _____
   _____
   _____

2. How are an ectopic pregnancy and a miscarriage similar? How are they different?
   _____
   _____
   _____
   _____
   _____
   _____

3. Why is it important for pregnant women to avoid alcohol, smoking, and drugs?
   _____
   _____
   _____
   _____
   _____
   _____

4. Distinguish between a vaginal delivery and a cesarean delivery of the fetus.
   _____
   _____
   _____
   _____
   _____

5. What four practical questions need to be answered when planning a family?
   _____
   _____
   _____
   _____
   _____
   _____

Name _____ Date _____ Class _____

Personal Inventory

Sexuality and Sexual Development

Thoughts and feelings about adolescence, sexuality, and sexual development can be confusing. To help clarify your own feelings and ideas, complete these statements. You do not need to let anyone else see your responses.

1. To me, sexuality means _____
_____
_____

2. Right now, my best source of information about human sexuality is _____
_____
_____

3. One thing about girls' physical development that I would like to know more about is
_____
_____

4. One thing about boys' physical development that I would like to know more about is
_____
_____

5. Talking about sexuality in different situations makes me feel
   (in class) _____
   (with my parents) _____
   (with close friends) _____

6. Problems that I think teenagers have about sexuality are _____
_____
_____

7. What I most look forward to learning about in this chapter is _____
_____
_____

8. I am not sure whether or not certain statements about sexuality and sexual development are true, such as _____
_____
_____

© Prentice-Hall, Inc.   Prentice Hall HEALTH: SKILLS FOR WELLNESS   37

Name _____ Date _____ Class _____

An Early Childhood Time Line

Practice

A child goes through various stages of mental and physical development. On the time line below, list some of the important mental and physical changes that occur in each stage of a child's development. Include information about the changing responsibilities of the parents. Some samples are provided.

To make the time line clear and easy to read, try using different colored pens or pencils for the different types of information.

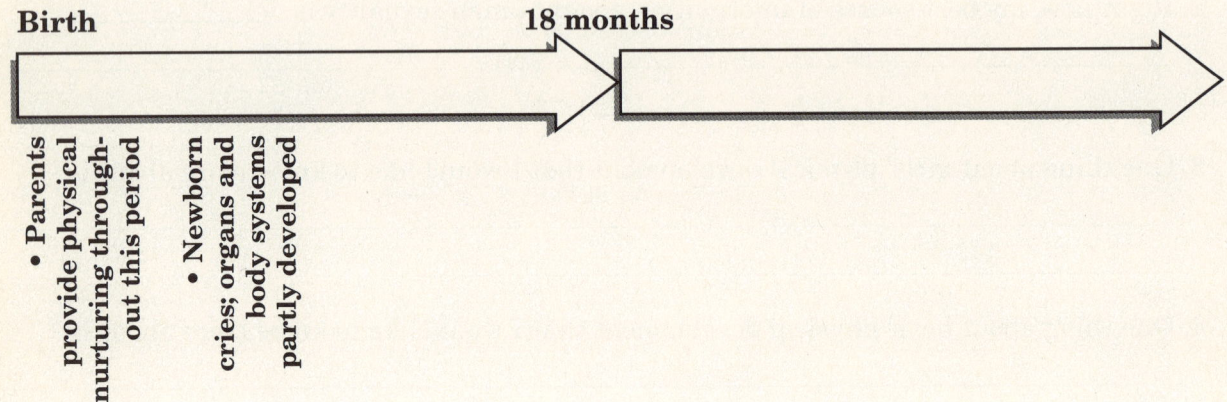

Birth → **18 months** →

- Parents provide physical nurturing throughout this period
- Newborn cries; organs and body systems partly developed

3 years → **6 years** → **12 years**

38   Prentice Hall HEALTH: SKILLS FOR WELLNESS   © Prentice-Hall, Inc.

Name _____ Date _____ Class _____

Chapter Review

Key Terms

Complete the following paragraph using the list of words and phrases below. Each word may be used once, more than once, or not at all. Then find and circle each word in the word search puzzle below.

peer pressure	values	late	self-esteem	autonomy
puberty	adolescence	secondary	identity	early
reproductive				

During ___(1)___ there is a gradual change from childhood to adulthood. A number of physical changes take place during this time. The release of sex hormones causes sexual maturation, or ___(2)___, as well as the development of ___(3)___ sex characteristics. Ovulation in girls and sperm production in boys signal ___(4)___ maturity. Adolescents who develop at a young age are sometimes called ___(5)___ bloomers. Those who develop at an older age are called ___(6)___ bloomers.

Mental, emotional, and social changes also take place during adolescence. Teenagers begin to question many things they previously accepted, such as the opinions and beliefs of others. This questioning helps adolescents discover their own ___(7)___, those beliefs and ideals that are important to them. An adolescent may also begin to ask questions and search for an ___(8)___, or an idea of who he or she is. This search is influenced by a person's ___(9)___, or how much a person likes himself or herself. The need to conform to the expectations of a person's friends, or ___(10)___, influences the way a person thinks he or she looks.

1. _____
2. _____
3. _____
4. _____
5. _____
6. _____
7. _____
8. _____
9. _____
10. _____

```
Q O R E P R O D U C T I V E
T A C R U V B O N W X C F A
X T J N B T Z H D V F N Q D
V K S S E C O N D A R Y W O
I G M V R L P I Q L R N F L
D S A B T Y C K Z U F C O E
E A R L Y W N E J E H S J S
N D H A X R V H S S T I Z C
T O V T E U M T L H N Y D E
I T S E L F E S T E E M T N
T P E E R P R E S S U R E C
Y G R H M B O T Y C M I G E
```

(Continued)

© Prentice-Hall, Inc.   Prentice Hall HEALTH: SKILLS FOR WELLNESS   39

Name _____

Chapter Review (Continued)

Main Ideas
Explain why each of the changes described below is taking place.

1. You notice hair growing under your arms, where you had none before. _____
   _____
   _____
   _____

2. You feel as if you are always hungry. There are aches and cramps in your arms and legs, and you have grown several inches in a few months. _____
   _____
   _____
   _____

3. You are beginning to think more about abstract ideas, such as the cause of world hunger. _____
   _____
   _____
   _____

4. You are beginning to question who you are and what you will do with your life.
   _____
   _____
   _____

5. On some days you want more independence about the clothes you wear and what you do with your free time. On other days, you wish you could hide your head under a pillow and let someone make all the decisions for you. _____
   _____
   _____
   _____

6. Lately, you have found it very satisfying to participate in community activities. _____
   _____
   _____
   _____

Name _____ Date _____ Class _____

Attitudes Toward Death and Dying

Personal Inventory

Dealing with ideas of death and dying is very difficult for most people. To identify some of your own ideas about these subjects, finish these sentences.

1. I think that death is _____
_____

2. What scares me most about death is _____
_____

3. If I knew I were going to die today, I would most regret _____
_____

4. I would rather die when _____
_____

5. If one of my friends' parents died, I would _____
_____

6. If someone close to me died, I would want my friends to help me by _____
_____

7. If a friend or relative were dying, I could help the person _____
_____

8. If someone I cared about died, I would feel _____
_____

9. If I were dying, I would like _____
_____

10. When I die, I would like to be remembered as _____
_____

What do your answers show you about your attitudes toward death and dying?
_____
_____

What feelings did you discover you had? _____
_____

What do these feelings tell you about your life? _____
_____

Name _____ Date _____ Class _____

 **Asking About Young Adulthood** *Practice*

You are now an adolescent. Have you thought about the next stage of your life? What will it be like to be a young adult? What kinds of issues will concern you? What kinds of changes will affect you?

Write a description of your life as a mature young adult between the ages of 20 and 40. Consider the physical and emotional changes you will experience. Include information about your work, your relationships, and your goals and achievements.

Physical changes: _____
_____
_____
_____

Emotional changes: _____
_____
_____
_____

Relationships: _____
_____
_____
_____

Occupation: _____
_____
_____
_____

Goals: _____
_____
_____
_____

Achievements: _____
_____
_____
_____

Chapter Review

Key Terms

Complete the following paragraphs using the list of words or phrases below. Each answer may be used once, more than once, or not at all.

emotional intimacy	generativity	Parkinson's disease	elasticity
climacteric	arthritis	immune system	hospice
terminal illness	dementia	osteoporosis	integrity
maturity	physical peak	validation	

People who are healthy and have had adequate nutrition and exercise are likely to reach their __(1)__ during young adulthood. Most people reach __(2)__, which is the state of being fully grown in the physical sense, at this stage of life. Young adults are more likely to form lasting friendships, because they have a better sense of who they are. Friends are a good source of __(3)__, the process of reassuring a person that his or her feelings, ideas, or decisions are reasonable.

Aging is a normal biological process. During middle adulthood, there is a gradual decrease in hormone production, called the __(4)__. Erik Erikson identifies __(5)__ as the central task of middle adulthood. This is the ability to care for others while maintaining self-esteem and personal identity.

Older adults show many physical changes. Their skin loses __(6)__, and their hair turns white. The __(7)__ is weakened, so illness from infectious diseases becomes more of a threat. Some older adults suffer from __(8)__, which is characterized by loss of mental abilities, abnormal behavior, and personality changes. People who have an illness that results in death have a __(9)__. A __(10)__ is a program that provides physical, emotional, and spiritual care for dying people and support for their families.

1. _____
2. _____
3. _____
4. _____
5. _____
6. _____
7. _____
8. _____
9. _____
10. _____

Supply the correct term to complete each sentence.

11. Achieving _____ means you feel content and are able to enjoy life.

12. Having a clear idea of who you are and trusting others are the basis for _____.

13. _____ is characterized by a progressive loss of normal muscle function.

14. A form of dementia caused by the degeneration of brain cells is called _____.

11. _____
12. _____
13. _____
14. _____

(Continued)

Name _____

Chapter Review (Continued)

Main Ideas
Answer each of the following questions.

1. What is the relationship between emotional intimacy and emotional maturity? _____
_____
_____
_____
_____
_____

2. Describe dementia and Alzheimer's disease. How are they related? _____
_____
_____
_____
_____
_____

3. Compare and contrast intimacy and integrity. How are they related? _____
_____
_____
_____
_____
_____

4. What is meant by the statement "Death is a part of life"? _____
_____
_____
_____
_____
_____

5. How has the process of dying changed? Why are people concerned about this change?
_____
_____
_____
_____

Name _____ Date _____ Class _____

Personal Inventory
Food Diary

A good way to get an accurate picture of what you eat is to keep a food diary. It will help you compare the number of recommended servings of each food type with what you eat.

In the first column of the table, record everything you eat in one day. Then make check marks to indicate what food group(s) each food belongs to. Be specific. For example, if you eat a tuna sandwich, list everything in it—bread, lettuce, tomato, mayonnaise, and tuna. At the end of the day, analyze your diet by totaling the number of servings you had from each group. The numbers in parentheses indicate the number of servings that you should be eating.

Food Groups and Recommended Daily Servings					
Foods Eaten	Grains (6–11)	Vegetables (3–5)	Fruit (2–4)	Milk and Milk Products (2–3)	Meats, Nuts, Legumes (2–3)	Fats, Oils, Sweets (sparingly)
Totals						

Compare what you ate with the recommended servings for each food group.

What should you eat less of? _____
_____
_____
_____

What should you eat more of? _____
_____
_____
_____

Name _____ Date _____ Class _____

Practice
12 Hunger and Malnutrition

Many people cannot meet their nutritional needs. They may not have enough food, or they may not get enough of the right kinds of foods. Hunger and malnutrition are serious problems worldwide.

Complete the diagram below by listing three causes of malnutrition, three effects of malnutrition, and three ways in which people attempt to solve the problem.

MALNUTRITION

Causes
- _____
- _____
- _____

Effects
- _____
- _____
- _____

Solutions
- _____
- _____
- _____

Name _____ Date _____ Class _____

Chapter Review

Key Terms

On the line at the left, write the letter of the word that matches each numbered description below. Each item may be used only once or not at all.

- **a.** cholesterol
- **b.** fiber
- **c.** glycogen
- **d.** carbohydrates
- **e.** glucose
- **f.** amino acids
- **g.** hemoglobin
- **h.** proteins

_____ 1. major type of sugar used by the body as an energy source

_____ 2. complex carbohydrate found in plants that is not digested

_____ 3. waxy, fatlike substance found in the cells of animals

_____ 4. group of nutrients that includes sugars and starches

_____ 5. nutrients that contain nitrogen as well as carbon, hydrogen, and oxygen

_____ 6. building blocks of protein

Complete the following paragraphs using the list of words below. Each word may be used once, more than once, or not at all.

- **a.** nutrient density
- **b.** glycogen
- **c.** malnutrition
- **d.** dehydration
- **e.** nutrients
- **f.** calories
- **g.** metabolism
- **h.** nutrition

The food you eat provides your body with energy. Your body breaks down the food and releases energy in the process called __(7)__. This energy is measured in units called __(8)__. You commonly eat more carbohydrates at a meal than your body can use immediately, so the extra glucose is converted into __(9)__, a type of starch.

As long as your body gets and uses adequate amounts of __(10)__, or substances it needs to grow and perform mentally and physically, it is receiving proper __(11)__. When a person's nutrient consumption is inadequate or unbalanced, that person may suffer from __(12)__. In this condition a person often lacks energy and is susceptible to disease.

7. _____
8. _____
9. _____
10. _____
11. _____
12. _____

(Continued)

Name _____

Chapter Review (Continued)

Main Ideas
Answer each of the following questions.

1. Explain the general ways in which your body uses nutrients in food. _____
   _____
   _____
   _____
   _____

2. Describe the benefits of a diet high in grains, vegetables, and fruits. _____
   _____
   _____
   _____
   _____

3. Describe the good and bad points of milk-group foods. _____
   _____
   _____
   _____
   _____

4. What is the relationship between saturated fats, cholesterol level, and heart disease?
   _____
   _____
   _____
   _____
   _____

5. Describe protein-energy malnutrition. What group is most affected? Why? _____
   _____
   _____
   _____
   _____

Name _____ Date _____ Class _____

Personal Inventory
Food Choices

Food choices are affected by many things—moods, surroundings, companions, feelings, and family background. What kinds of foods do you usually choose in each of these situations?

1. When I am home sick with a cold,
   I usually eat _____

2. When I am eating out with friends,
   I usually eat _____

3. When I am in a hurry for breakfast,
   I usually eat _____

4. When I have plenty of time for breakfast,
   I usually eat _____

5. When I eat lunch at school,
   I usually eat _____

6. When I eat lunch at home on weekends,
   I usually eat _____

7. When I am bored or depressed,
   I usually eat _____

8. When there is a special family celebration,
   I usually eat _____

9. When I have a test or important game the next day,
   I usually eat _____

How do certain situations influence your food choices? _____
_____
_____

Do any of your choices include foods that reflect special traditions or family background?
Which ones? _____
_____
_____
_____
_____

Name _____ Date _____ Class _____

Practice
Improving Your Diet

Work through this exercise in pairs to learn about healthy diets.

1. Make a set of pink 3 x 5 cards, each with one of the following lesson concepts written on it:

how people decide what to eat	lunch	ways to improve the diet
fast-food restaurants	breakfast	older adults' nutritional needs
adolescents' nutritional needs	supper	snacks

2. Make a set of white 3 x 5 cards, each with one of the following words or phrases written on it:

culture	peer pressure
personal preferences	increased intake of fiber
fruit, bagel, popcorn	ample levels of protein
salad bar instead of French fries	cafeterias offer nutritional alternatives
economic situation	significant amounts of iron
fuel for rest of the day's activities	juice, not shakes
choose foods low in fats or sugars	meal for filling in the day's nutrients
use salt and sodium in moderation	choose a variety of foods
grilled chicken sandwich, not hamburger	need for calcium
feature meals high in fat and calories	no more than one-third daily food needs
day's most important meal, according to many nutritionists	choose lots of vegetables, fruits, and grain products

3. In this exercise each white card supports one or more lesson concepts. When it is your turn, place each white supporting card beneath the appropriate pink concept card. Your partner can ask you to explain any of your choices, and to suggest which white cards may fit under more than one concept card.

After you and your partner have worked through the exercise, answer the following questions:

1. How can you choose a nutritious meal at a fast-food restaurant? _____
   _____

2. In terms of nutrients, what special characteristics describe each of the three meals of the day?

   Breakfast: _____
   Lunch: _____
   Supper: _____

Name _____ Date _____ Class _____

Chapter Review

Key Terms
Use the clues to identify the terms. Then find the terms in the word search puzzle below.

1. chemicals that prevent food spoilage
2. a kind of additive that keeps fats from separating from other ingredients in a food
3. estimate of how long a product is usable
4. refraining from eating all foods for a period of time
5. desire for food based on emotional factors rather than nutritional need
6. condition of being 20 percent or more above an appropriate weight
7. description of food to which vitamins, minerals, or proteins have been added
8. popular diet for weight loss that disregards proper nutrition and other matters of health
9. low blood sugar
10. rate at which the body uses energy when at complete rest
11. substance that allows glucose to pass from the blood into the body's cells
12. cost per unit of measurement

1. _____
2. _____
3. _____
4. _____
5. _____
6. _____
7. _____
8. _____
9. _____
10. _____
11. _____
12. _____

```
R B A S A L M E T A B O L I C R A T E
S Y P R O D U C T D A T E I K B N O F
P R E S E R V A T I V E S N R N T J O
Q E C D S C R A T C H T E S T L E M F
N H A P D P O Y R C V H B U M N M J A
A Y T P T S A Q R Z N I V L K X U O D
L P Y D E H P M O O B E S I T Y L I D
S O X O W M P P I M J G H N E P S Q I
T G Z N Q F E P R E K E R V J T I Q E
R L H U N I T P R I C E T D L V F N T
Y Y U N J Q I Z I T F L U C T E I F G
Z C G R V R T S B I A D E I E S E R Y
B E T V P Y E A S J S H I K G M R K H
A M B E D K V F O R T I F I E D G Q B
O I W S X U T C G S I F R R Q F L C M
I A A N O R E X I A N E R V O S A Z A
S J W F D V G X H E G B P Y A D N E O
```

(Continued)

© Prentice-Hall, Inc.   Prentice Hall HEALTH: SKILLS FOR WELLNESS   51

Name _____

Chapter Review (Continued)

Main Ideas
Answer each of the following questions on the lines provided.

1. A young man has high blood pressure and needs to reduce his salt intake. How can he find out approximately how much salt is in different packaged foods? _____
   _____
   _____

2. Your friend's mother is pregnant. Your friend is helping her plan a diet that will be best for her and her baby. What guidelines should they follow? Why? _____
   _____
   _____

3. A teenage boy has been feeling very thirsty, and even though his appetite is good, he is still losing weight. He also feels tired and irritable. Tests show a high level of sugar in his blood. What problem may he have? Describe a diet for him if he has that condition.
   _____
   _____

4. A teenage girl has been trying to lose weight. However, she abandons her weight reduction program whenever she becomes unhappy or bored. What advice could you give her?
   _____
   _____

5. A 14-year-old boy wants to lose weight by fasting. Explain to him why this is not a good idea. _____
   _____
   _____

6. A teenage girl has decided to become a strict vegetarian. She plans to eliminate dairy products and eggs. How can she be sure her diet includes all the essential amino acids?
   _____
   _____
   _____

7. A woman has hypoglycemia. What kind of diet should she eat? _____
   _____
   _____
   _____

Prentice Hall HEALTH: SKILLS FOR WELLNESS   © Prentice-Hall, Inc.

Name _____ Date _____ Class _____

Personal Inventory
Healthy Mealtimes

There is more to mealtimes than just enjoying what you eat. In fact, a healthy digestive system relies on two things—what you eat and how you eat. You can learn about your own habits by filling out this inventory.

1. Some of my favorite kinds of foods are _____
   _____
   _____

2. Some of my *least* favorite kinds of foods are _____
   _____
   _____

3. I drink these beverages with my meals: _____
   _____

4. I spend this much time eating each meal: breakfast _____
   lunch _____
   supper _____

5. The people I eat my meals with are _____
   _____

6. At mealtime we talk about _____
   _____

Choose one of the items in parentheses or fill in the blank.

7. If I eat alone, I usually (watch TV, listen to the radio, read) or _____

8. After I eat my meals, I take care of my teeth by _____

9. Most of my mealtimes are (relaxed or stressful) because _____
   _____

Read through your answers. Indicate which of your habits you think are good ones. Explain how you think you can change your habits to make yourself healthier.

_____
_____
_____
_____

© Prentice-Hall, Inc.   Prentice Hall HEALTH: SKILLS FOR WELLNESS

Name _____ Date _____ Class _____

14 Steps in the Digestive Process

Practice

As soon as food enters your body, it begins the process of digestion.

Use the lines below to write a short description of what happens to a piece of food as it moves through each step in the digestive process. Be sure to include both the mechanical and the chemical process at each stage. Inside the outline of the person below, draw a diagram of the digestive process to accompany your description. Be sure to label the parts of the digestive system in your diagram.

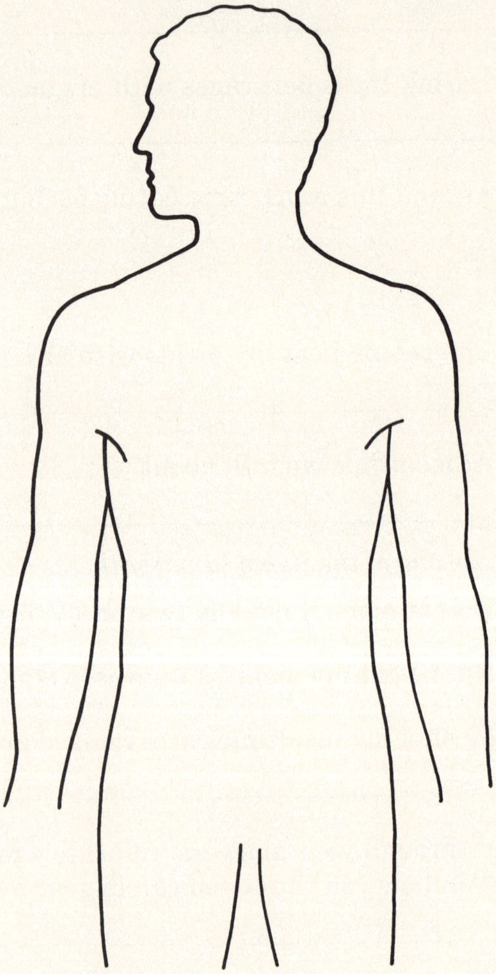

_____
_____
_____
_____
_____
_____
_____
_____
_____
_____
_____
_____
_____
_____
_____
_____
_____
_____
_____
_____

Prentice Hall HEALTH: SKILLS FOR WELLNESS © Prentice-Hall, Inc.

Chapter Review

Key Terms
Complete the crossword puzzle below.

Across
3. organs that filter wastes, particularly urea, from the bloodstream
4. poisoning caused by kidney failure
6. muscular, saclike organ that produces gastric juices
9. flap of tissue that covers the windpipe
10. substances that help carry out chemical reactions in the body
11. a condition in which the gums become red and swollen and bleed easily

Down
1. muscular tube connecting the mouth and the stomach
2. waste product containing nitrogen that is produced by breakdown of protein
5. channel in tooth through which nerves and blood vessels pass
7. tiny, fingerlike projections in the small intestine that absorb substances into the bloodstream
8. most of the tooth consists of this yellowish bonelike material

(Continued)

Name _____

Chapter Review (Continued)

Main Ideas
Answer each of the following questions.

1. What happens to your teeth when plaque is not removed regularly? _____
_____
_____
_____
_____
_____

2. If someone has an untreated malocclusion, what problems can he or she have? _____
_____
_____
_____
_____
_____

3. Describe digestion in the mouth and digestion in the small intestine. _____
_____
_____
_____
_____
_____

4. How is liver function important for digestion? _____
_____
_____
_____
_____
_____

5. What condition is produced by prolonged diarrhea? What signs indicate that medical attention is needed? _____
_____
_____
_____
_____
_____

Name _____ Date _____ Class _____

Personal Inventory

Healthy Bones, Muscles, and Nerves

There are a number of steps that you can take to ensure that your bones, muscles, and nerves are being cared for in healthy ways. Consider the following healthy choices. How often do you make them a part of your life? Put checks in the appropriate columns.

Fitness Choices

Healthy Choices	Always	Usually	Sometimes	Seldom/Never
1. I eat foods high in calcium, such as milk products; dark green, leafy vegetables; tofu; legumes.				
2. I eat well-balanced meals.				
3. I exercise regularly.				
4. I do warm-up/cool-down and stretching exercises when I work out.				
5. I get 8 hours of sleep at night.				
6. I refuse to use alcohol.				
7. I use a safety belt when riding in a car.				
8. I wear a helmet when I ride a bicycle or motorcycle or play contact sports.				
9. I refuse to use illegal drugs, including anabolic steroids.				
10. I avoid injuring muscles by not putting too much stress on them.				

Review your responses. In what ways can you improve your choices?
_____
_____

Indicate your favorite form of exercise. List the kinds of risks that are part of that activity and choices you can make to reduce those risks.
_____
_____

© Prentice-Hall, Inc.   Prentice Hall HEALTH: SKILLS FOR WELLNESS

Name _____ Date _____ Class _____

15 The Way Muscles Work
Practice

Understanding muscles—the different types, how they work, their disorders, and what keeps them healthy—is essential to your health.

Look at the pictures below. Then answer the questions next to each picture.

When Matsumi uses her leg muscles to run, which of the three types of muscles is she using: skeletal, smooth, or cardiac? Are these muscle movements voluntary or involuntary?

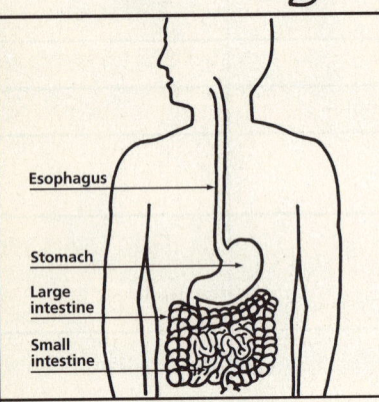

When food moves through the digestive system organs indicated by the arrows, which type of muscles are being used? Are these muscle movements voluntary or involuntary?

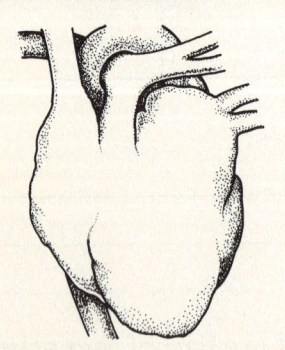

When the heart pumps blood, which kind of muscles are being used? Are these muscle movements voluntary or involuntary?

When you eat your dinner, you lift the food to your mouth, chew it, swallow it, and digest it. Explain how all three types of muscles are being used during this process.

_____
_____
_____

58   Prentice Hall HEALTH: SKILLS FOR WELLNESS   © Prentice-Hall, Inc.

Name _____ Date _____ Class _____

Chapter Review

Key Terms

On the line at the right, write the word or phrase that matches each numbered description below. Each answer may be used once, more than once, or not at all.

cerebellum	cartilage	epilepsy	fracture
lactic acid	cerebrum	coma	joint
reflex	muscle tone	marrow	osteoporosis
meninges	ossification	dendrites	concussion
somatic nervous system	migraine	axial skeleton	appendicular skeleton
brainstem	tendons	hypothalamus	
	ligaments		

1. condition characterized by a sudden storm of brain activity resulting in a seizure 1._____
2. break in a bone 2._____
3. large upper region of the brain 3._____
4. waste product that accumulates in muscles during intense exercise, when muscles do not get enough oxygen 4._____
5. point at which two bones come together 5._____
6. slight, constant contraction of a muscle 6._____
7. condition in which bones become weak and break easily 7._____
8. deposition of minerals within the cartilage 8._____
9. thick strands of connective tissue that attach skeletal muscles to bones 9._____
10. the part of the peripheral nervous system responsible for actions that you can control 10._____
11. especially severe headache that usually lasts a long time; may be caused by the changing diameter of blood vessels 11._____
12. tough supportive tissue that makes the backbone flexible and absorbs shocks 12._____
13. area of the brain that is the body's life-support system 13._____
14. prolonged period of deep unconsciousness 14._____
15. part of the brain that regulates body temperature, sleep, water balance, and blood pressure 15._____
16. soft tissue that fills the spaces inside bones 16._____
17. short, branching fibers that carry nerve impulses toward the nerve cell body 17._____

(Continued)

© Prentice-Hall, Inc.   Prentice Hall HEALTH: SKILLS FOR WELLNESS

Name _____

Chapter Review (Continued)

18. three layers of membranes that cover and protect the brain   18. _____
19. fibrous bands that hold bones together   19. _____
20. short loss of consciousness following head injury   20. _____

Main Ideas
Answer each of the following questions.

1. Compare the central nervous system and peripheral nervous system. How are they alike? How are they different?
   _____
   _____
   _____

2. Describe three ways you can develop a healthy muscular system.
   _____
   _____
   _____

3. Compare cartilage and bone. How are they alike? How are they different? Give an example of each.
   _____
   _____
   _____

Complete the chart below by supplying the information described in each column heading.

Division of Skeleton	Bones in Skeleton	Functions
4. Axial		
5. Appendicular		

60   Prentice Hall HEALTH: SKILLS FOR WELLNESS   © Prentice-Hall, Inc.

Name _____ Date _____ Class _____

Personal Inventory

Choices for Healthy Heart and Lungs

As you breathe in and out, oxygen is being sent through your respiratory and cardiovascular systems. Both of these systems work closely together. What do you do to keep them healthy? Your answers to the following statements should guide you in making healthy choices for your heart and lungs.

Breathing Clean Air

When sanding wood or working on a project that generates particles of dirt and dust into the air, I _____

When someone near me lights up a cigarette, I _____

When using paints or other solvents with strong fumes, I _____

Other steps I take to ensure I am breathing clean air include _____

Eating Healthy Foods

I eat lots of _____ to provide my body with adequate sources of iron. (See Figure 12-9, "Essential Minerals," in the text, page 276, for foods that are good sources of iron.)

To maintain a reasonable weight, I _____

I limit the fried foods I eat by substituting _____

I also reduce my intake of foods high in saturated fats and cholesterol by _____

Exercising

To relieve stress through exercise, I _____

The types of exercises I like to do are _____

© Prentice-Hall, Inc.   Prentice Hall HEALTH: SKILLS FOR WELLNESS

Name _____ Date _____ Class _____

Practice

Learning About Cardiovascular Disease

There are many kinds of cardiovascular disorders. To help you learn the names of the ones discussed in Lesson 3, fill in the name of the appropriate cardiovascular disorder on the line following each of the definitions given below.

1. a condition in which cholesterol and other fatty materials build up on artery walls
2. the condition that occurs when the coronary arteries become blocked as the result of a buildup of cholesterol and other fatty materials inside the coronary arteries
3. the chest pain that occurs when the flow of oxygen to the heart is reduced
4. the condition that results when some of the tissue in the heart is prevented from receiving its normal blood supply and dies
5. a structural problem of the heart that is present at birth
6. damage to the valves of the heart caused by rheumatic fever

1. _____
2. _____
3. _____
4. _____
5. _____
6. _____

Find the terms defined above among the letters in the box below. The terms may read backwards or upside down.

```
M B R N O P Q A B L F G H E L Q S E K J X R E
P A F G G A C B A B Z I B I H O T F P Q Y E F
R L I U H J D O R K I T A R S L I D L I Z M G
O R E L I L M A T O P H E M H D O K V E R F E
O H B N J O L O Q U K P A M R B U Q L C A M D
S E C M E B L H I U N F B N I G P H V U I O G
N U D F F V P F W P O C C O N K S P W Q T G A
A M O Q E R O A N G I N A P E C T O R I S C W
B A P E S A X T T S I B O Q O A P A Y P P T X
S T I K H T A S B L R K X R O T Q L S Q L H I
L I R L P H I Q Z H C L G F N T U M J N M I B
L C S M O E H D D N A G M I M A Z E L R N J R
U H T C O R O N A R Y H E A R T D I S E A S E
K E J A R O I L P Q U I V W F R E C M M T O O
J A U N J S K J X F M J O J K A R O Q N V D A
V R O X Y C Z O C R S T N X O E S E N I W A M
E T W O X L C Y Z L E O K U V H W G X O O N N
Y D F P I E P Q V O Q J M L T K A H O P I Q C
B I G A H R R B J L I O D Q U A R M P A C Q D
L S K Z J O N O Y Z E M C F V G E I Q H I P J
R E D R O S I D T R A E H L A T I N E G N O C
M A O N J I H N G K Y N D B W R F J L A E Y I
U S O I K S I D L H Z M E T X S G K I N F O I
Z E A P Q R N O P F G H E I L M H L A C D B X
```

Name _____ Date _____ Class _____

Chapter Review

Key Terms
Match each word with its correct definition.

sinuses	influenza	pneumonia	tuberculosis	cilia
lungs	bronchitis	atherosclerosis	atria	bronchi
diaphragm	ventricles	capillaries	blood pressure	asthma
platelets	hypertension	anemia	trachea	aorta

1. inflammation and swelling of the mucous membranes that line the bronchi _____

2. chambers of the heart that receive blood from either the lungs or the rest of the body _____

3. cartilage-ringed tubes that go from the trachea to each lung _____

4. blood pressure that is consistently higher than normal _____

5. pathway through which air moves from the pharynx into the chest _____

6. tiny, hairlike structures that line the air passages _____

7. hollow spaces above the nasal cavity _____

8. chambers of the heart that pump blood either to the lungs or to the rest of the body _____

9. pieces of cells that start the process of blood clotting _____

10. respiratory disorder in which the air passages become narrower than normal _____

11. large, elastic, spongy organs through which the body absorbs oxygen _____

12. largest artery in the body _____

13. force with which blood pushes against the walls of the blood vessels _____

14. buildup of cholesterol and other fatty materials on artery walls _____

15. main muscle involved in breathing; lies just below the lungs _____

16. serious infection in which fluids collect in the alveoli _____

17. condition in which there are too few red blood cells or too little hemoglobin in the blood _____

(Continued)

Name _____

Chapter Review (Continued)

18. respiratory infection with symptoms such as fever, headache, muscle aches, sore throat, and cough _____

19. smallest blood vessels in the body _____

20. long-term bacterial disease that affects the lungs and other parts of the body _____

Main Ideas
Answer each of the following questions.

1. Name the liquid and solid parts of the blood, and describe the functions of each part.
   _____
   _____
   _____

2. Describe three ways you can protect your respiratory and cardiovascular systems.
   _____
   _____

3. How are arteries and veins alike? How are they different? _____
   _____
   _____

Complete the chart below by supplying the information described in each column heading.

Type of Circulation	Pathway of Blood	Function
4. Pulmonary		
5. Systemic		

Name _____ Date _____ Class _____

Personal Inventory
Aspects of Fitness

Look at the chart. For each activity, the four areas of fitness are rated from 1 to 4. (Note the rating scale below the chart.) Read the list of activities and circle the ones that you do. Then answer the questions following the chart.

Fitness Ratings of Physical Activities				
Activity	Cardiorespiratory Endurance	Muscular Strength	Muscular Endurance	Flexibility
Aerobic dancing	3–4	2	2	3
Ballet	3	2	2	4
Baseball/Softball	1	1	1	2
Basketball	3–4	1	2	2
Bicycling (at least 10 mph)	3–4	2	3–4	1
Bowling	1	1	1	2
Calisthenics	3	3–4	3–4	3–4
Football	2–3	2	2	2
Gymnastics	1	4	3	4
Handball/Squash	3	2	3	2
Hiking (uphill)	3	1	2	2
Hockey	2–3	2	2	2
Jogging/Running (at least 6 mph)	3–4	1	3	2
Judo/Karate	1	2	1	3
Jumping Rope	3–4	1	3	2
Racquetball	3–4	1	3	2
Rowing	3–4	3	3	2
Skating (ice, roller)	2–3	1	2–3	2
Skiing (cross-country)	4	2	3–4	2
Skiing (downhill)	3	2	2–3	2
Soccer	3	2	2	2
Swimming	4	2	3	2
Tennis/Badminton (singles)	2–3	1	2–3	2
Volleyball	2	1	2	2
Walking (brisk)	3	1	3	2
Weight training	1–2	4	3	2
Wrestling	3–4	2	3	3
Rating Scale: 1 = Low, 2 = Moderate, 3 = High, 4 = Very High				

Which circled activity has the highest rating for cardiorespiratory endurance? For muscular strength? For flexibility? _____

How can you change your activities to increase your overall fitness? _____

© Prentice-Hall, Inc.   Prentice Hall HEALTH: SKILLS FOR WELLNESS

Name _____ Date _____ Class _____

Practice

Healthy Sleep

Sleep is vital for good health. During this state of deep relaxation, the body renews itself. Reread the section on page 411 of the text entitled "How Much Sleep Is Enough?" Then answer the following questions.

1. Why is a nighttime routine important? _____
   _____

2. Should you go to bed at about the same time on weekends as you do during the week? Why or why not? _____
   _____

3. Why should you not have music or a light on when you are sleeping? _____
   _____

4. Why do infants and adolescents need more sleep than other people do? _____
   _____

Fill in the chart below with four tips that would be helpful in getting a good night's sleep. Then cut the rows out and arrange them in order, according to which ones you find easiest to follow. Compare your tips and rankings with those of your classmates.

Tips for a Good Night's Sleep

66 Prentice Hall HEALTH: SKILLS FOR WELLNESS

Name _____ Date _____ Class _____

Chapter Review

Key Terms

Complete the following paragraphs using the list of words below. Each word may be used once, more than once, or not at all.

cool-down	flexibility	endorphins	cardiorespiratory endurance
isometric	aerobic	isokinetic	body composition
anaerobic	warm-up	isotonic	muscle strength and endurance

Fitness has four health-related components. The ability of the heart, blood vessels, and lungs to distribute nutrients and oxygen and remove waste is __(1)__ . The ability of muscles to resist a force and work for an extended period of time is __(2)__ . The ability to use a muscle's full range of motion is called __(3)__ ; __(4)__ is the amount of body fat compared to lean tissue.

Exercise has many physical and psychological benefits. It strengthens the heart and builds muscle strength. It also produces a sense of satisfaction and pleasure, partly from the release of natural substances called __(5)__ that give a feeling of well-being.

Exercises that increase the amount of oxygen that is taken in and used by the body are __(6)__ . Exercises that cause the muscles to use up much more oxygen than the blood can supply are __(7)__ . Running and dancing are examples of __(8)__ exercise because they improve your cardiovascular and respiratory systems. Anaerobic exercises, however, are intense workouts that increase strength and endurance of muscles. Exercises that make use of special types of weight-training machines are __(9)__ . Bending and straightening the arm, thereby causing contraction and relaxation of the arm muscles through the full range of their motion, is a(n) __(10)__ exercise. Pushing hard against a wall is an example of a(n) __(11)__ exercise.

When deciding on an exercise program, people need to take into account their own interests, abilities, and needs. Every fitness program should include a(n) __(12)__ , five to ten minutes of mild exercise to prepare the body for vigorous exercise, followed by a stretching period. After a vigorous workout, it is necessary to go through a(n) __(13)__ period of milder exercise for about ten minutes so that the body can return to its resting state slowly. Walking is a good way to do that.

1. _____
2. _____
3. _____
4. _____
5. _____
6. _____
7. _____
8. _____
9. _____
10. _____
11. _____
12. _____
13. _____

Define or describe the following terms.

14. NREM sleep _____

15. sleep apnea _____

16. narcolepsy _____

(Continued)

Name _____

Chapter Review (Continued)

Main Ideas
Answer each of the following questions.

1. José wants to build up his overall muscle strength but he can afford neither the fees at the nearby fitness center nor the cost of an elaborate weight-lifting kit. Recommend an exercise program that will help him achieve his goals. _____
_____
_____
_____

2. Sally is over 30, and her doctor has warned her that she may develop osteoporosis. Why would exercise be beneficial to her? _____
_____
_____
_____

3. Henry has finally recovered from an illness that kept him in bed for almost three months. Now he needs an exercise program that will rebuild his cardiovascular and respiratory endurance. What type of exercise would help him achieve this goal? _____
_____
_____

Name four physical activities that are forms of this type of exercise. _____
_____
_____
_____

4. Julie likes to begin exercising vigorously without any warm-up. What would you say to convince her that she needs to warm up? _____
_____
_____
_____

5. Tim, who is 15, asks how many hours of sleep he should be getting and what the best conditions for sleep are. What would you tell him? _____
_____
_____
_____

Name _____ Date _____ Class _____

Personal Inventory
Personal Care Products

When you go to buy shampoo or any other personal care product, you confront shelf after shelf of choices. Most people have many reasons for making choices like this. The product must do the job, of course. But there are other reasons as well. Use this inventory to discover how you choose.

1. The package of a personal care product usually contains some information about the product—its price, the ingredients, instructions for use, and so on. For each of the following types of products, indicate the kinds of information you find most useful.

   Shampoo _____

   Hair conditioner _____

   Soap _____

   Sunscreen _____

   Sunglasses _____

   Skin medication _____

   Dry-skin lotion _____

   Other _____

2. What other things about a product appeal to you? Maybe you are responding to advertising, an endorsement from a celebrity, or choices made by your friends or family. For each of the following products, check off the appeals that influence your choices.

Product	Advertising	Endorsement	Friends	Family
Shampoo				
Hair conditioner				
Soap				
Sunscreen				
Sunglasses				
Skin medication				
Dry-skin lotion				
Other				

3. Look over your answers to questions 1 and 2. What considerations are most important when you buy a personal care product? _____

_____

4. What information would help you be a wiser consumer of health-care products?

_____

© Prentice-Hall, Inc.   Prentice Hall HEALTH: SKILLS FOR WELLNESS

Name _____ Date _____ Class _____

Practice
How the Ear Works

Sound waves travel through the three main parts of the ear before reaching the brain as nerve impulses, enabling us to hear. The ear also helps us maintain balance.

Copy the parts of the ear listed below onto a piece of paper, cut them out, and mix them up. Then reorder them to reflect the structure of the ear. Write a paragraph explaining the process of how the ear works to process sound waves and maintain the body's sense of balance. Use the ordered cards to help organize your paragraph.

Outer Ear	Middle Ear	Inner Ear
collecting funnel	hammer	oval window of the cochlea
ear canal	anvil	fluid in the coiled tube of the cochlea
glands in the skin lining the ear canal	stirrup	vibration-sensing cells lining the cochlea
eardrum	eustachian tube	nerves connected to the cells lining the cochlea
		auditory nerve
		semicircular canals

70 Prentice Hall HEALTH: SKILLS FOR WELLNESS   © Prentice-Hall, Inc.

Name _____ Date _____ Class _____

Chapter Review

Key Terms
Match each structure on the left with its correct function on the right.

_____ 1. cochlea
_____ 2. semicircular canals
_____ 3. dermis
_____ 4. pore
_____ 5. pupil
_____ 6. lens
_____ 7. herpes simplex I
_____ 8. retina
_____ 9. melanin
_____ 10. cornea

a. detect changes in body position
b. opening of a narrow channel, or duct, that leads to a gland in the skin
c. regulates amount of light entering the eye
d. substance that is a major factor in determining the color of the skin
e. focuses light on the inner back side of the eye
f. light-sensing part of the eye
g. contains blood vessels that bring nutrients to the skin and carry away waste products
h. allows light to enter the eye
i. causes clusters of watery blisters, or cold sores, usually around the mouth
j. contains special vibration-sensing cells that send nerve signals to the brain

Use the clue to help unscramble each of the following words below. Write the correct answer in the space.

11. SAREMTODILOGT — doctor who handles skin problems — 11. _____

12. DISPEREMI — outermost layer of the skin — 12. _____

13. SDEREGENSNAITHS — vision problem in which a person cannot see objects that are far away — 13. _____

14. USOCEASEB — type of gland that produces oil — 14. _____

15. BECEDIL — unit used to measure loudness of sound — 15. _____

16. RACLES — white outside layer of the eye — 16. _____

17. LEMMANAO — skin cancer that can spread to other organs of the body — 17. _____

(Continued)

© Prentice-Hall, Inc.   Prentice Hall HEALTH: SKILLS FOR WELLNESS   71

Name _____

Chapter Review (Continued)

Main Ideas
Write the letters on the diagrams to label correctly the following structures.

    a. sclera   **d.** lens   **g.** anvil   **j.** eustachian tube
    b. optic nerve   **e.** pupil   **h.** eardrum   **k.** cochlea
    c. cornea   **f.** retina   **i.** stirrup   **l.** ear canal

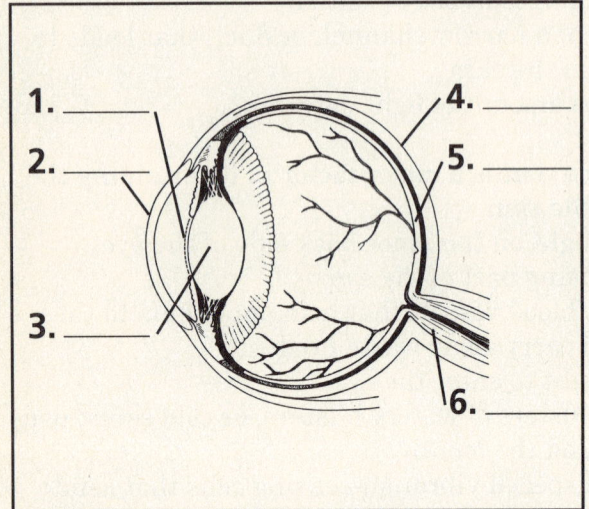
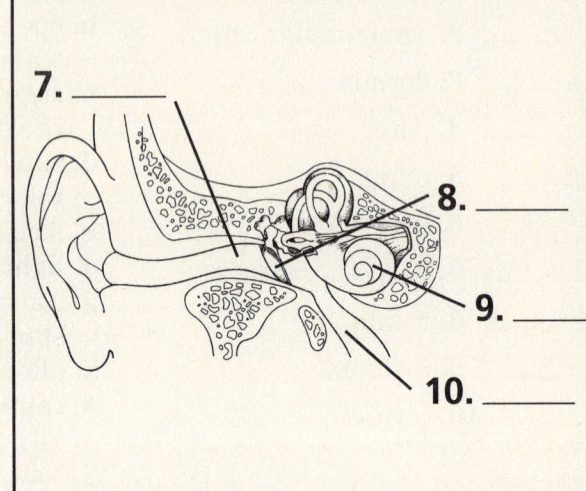

Complete the chart below by describing the symptoms, cause, and prevention of each health problem.

Problem	Symptoms	Cause	Prevention
Acne			
Cataract			
Athlete's foot			
Torn eardrum			

Name _____ Date _____ Class _____

Personal Inventory
Attitudes Toward Alcohol

Both teenagers and adults hold many different attitudes toward alcohol and its use. To look more closely at your own attitudes and behavior, complete these sentences. Finish these sentences with your opinions.

1. People drink alcohol when _____
   _____

2. Controlling the use of alcohol is _____
   _____

3. Getting drunk _____
   _____

4. When it comes to alcohol, my friends _____
   _____

5. Among my friends, the pressure to have a drink _____
   _____

6. Running ads for alcohol on TV sports programs _____
   _____

Describe what you would do in each of these situations.

1. I am at a party where a lot of beer, wine, and liquor is being served.
   I would _____

2. A good friend has been drinking a lot and is about to have another beer.
   I would _____

3. My friends are pressuring me to have "just one drink."
   I would _____

4. I am at a party where I know only a few people, and I am feeling uncomfortable.
   I would _____

5. A friend tells me one of her (or his) parents is an alcoholic.
   I would _____

Look over your responses. Are there any attitudes or behaviors you would change? If so, which ones? _____
_____

© Prentice-Hall, Inc.   Prentice Hall HEALTH: SKILLS FOR WELLNESS

Name _____ Date _____ Class _____

19 Alcohol's Effects on the Body

Practice

Intoxication affects nearly every part of the body. Some effects of intoxication are short-term and some are long-term. Follow the directions below to make a visual representation of how alcohol affects the body. Use red pencil to mark short-term effects and blue pencil to mark long-term effects.

Short-term effects of alcohol abuse:

1. When the liver cannot break down alcohol as fast as it enters the body, intoxication results. *Draw stripes* across the liver.
2. Alcohol reduces sensation and muscle coordination, which are controlled by the brain. *Circle* the brain.
3. The brain and the stomach are affected by a hangover. *Draw a star* inside each of these organs.
4. Excess alcohol may cause the kidneys to release too much water from the body. *Draw dots* inside the kidneys.
5. A blood alcohol concentration (BAC) of 0.40 to 0.50 can cause breathing and heart action to stop. *Mark the letter X* over the lungs and heart.

Long-term effects of alcohol abuse:

6. The mouth, throat, esophagus, and tongue are at an increased risk of cancer. *Mark the letter C* over these organs.
7. The liver is damaged by alcohol so that it cannot break down fats. *Mark the letter D* for "damaged" over the liver.
8. Alcohol abuse contributes to heart disease. *Shade in* the heart.

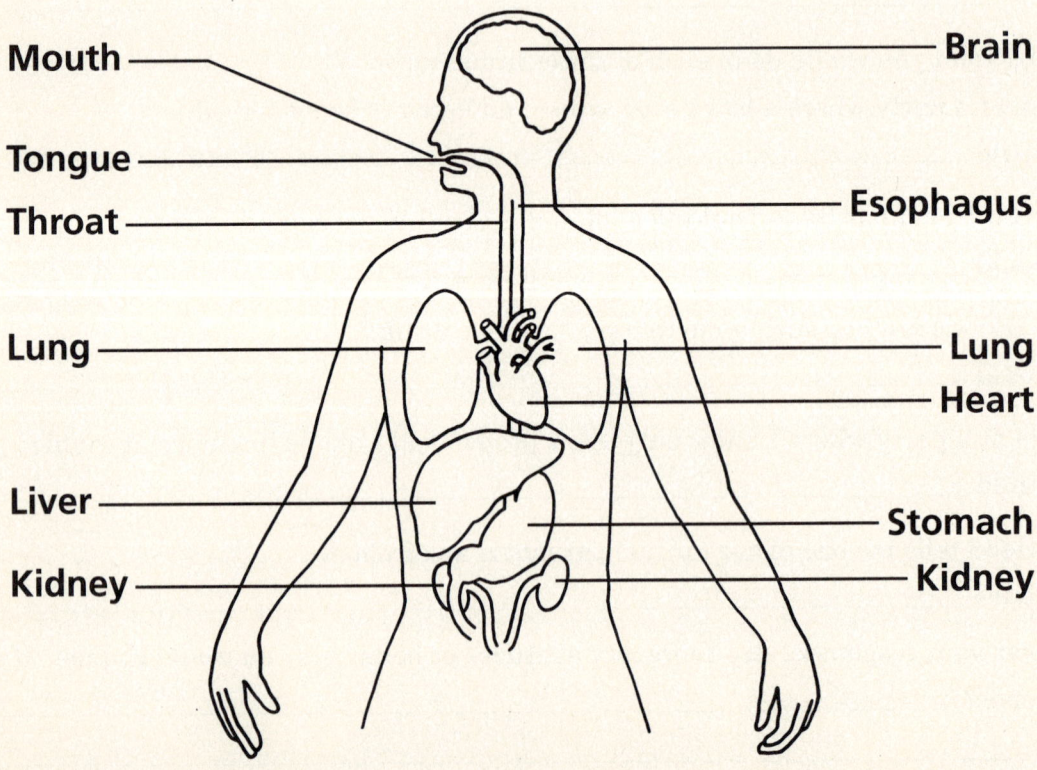

74 Prentice Hall HEALTH: SKILLS FOR WELLNESS © Prentice-Hall, Inc.

Chapter Review

Key Terms

Complete the following paragraphs using the list of words or phrases below. Each answer may be used once, more than once, or not at all.

refusal skills	depressant	rehabilitation
synergism	withdrawal	abstains
ethanol	intoxication	tolerance
delirium tremens	Alcoholics Anonymous	intervention
cirrhosis	alcoholism	detoxification
fetal alcohol syndrome	inhibitions	

__(1)__ is the powerful drug in beverages such as beer, wine, and liquor. It acts as a __(2)__, which slows the central nervous system. __(3)__ refers to the many negative effects of drinking alcohol, which include blurred vision, slurred speech, and impaired coordination.

Pregnant women who drink put the health of their children at risk. Drinking alcohol is the leading preventable cause of mental retardation, which is just one of the birth defects caused by the disorder called __(4)__.

Over time, a heavy drinker's body becomes accustomed to, or develops a __(5)__ for, alcohol, and requires increasingly large amounts to achieve the original effect. __(6)__ of the liver is a disease in which scar tissue from dead, fat-filled cells replaces healthy tissue and causes the liver to fail.

Alcohol has behavioral as well as physical effects. When people drink, they lose their __(7)__, or the control they normally put on their emotions.

Drinkers who are addicted to alcohol suffer from the disease called __(8)__. Without alcohol, the alcoholic experiences __(9)__, which is characterized by shakiness, sleep problems, irritability, a rapid heartbeat, and sweating. In the late stage of alcoholism, a severe reaction of the central nervous system to the absence of alcohol called __(10)__ can occur, sometimes resulting in death.

After acknowledging their problem and asking for help, alcoholics can move to the next step, recovery. __(11)__ is the removal of alcohol from the person's body. After achieving a sober state, the alcoholic begins __(12)__, the process of learning to cope with the stress of everyday living without alcohol. Many recovering alcoholics belong to support groups such as __(13)__, where they can share their struggles and build healthy relationships.

One in every three Americans chooses not to drink, or __(14)__ from, alcohol. It is hard to resist peer pressure and advertising, but many people who choose not to drink develop __(15)__ to help them say *no* confidently.

1. _____
2. _____
3. _____
4. _____
5. _____
6. _____
7. _____
8. _____
9. _____
10. _____
11. _____
12. _____
13. _____
14. _____
15. _____

(Continued)

Name _____

Chapter Review (Continued)

Main Ideas
Answer each of the following questions.

1. The early stage of alcoholism is characterized by problem drinking. What are the behaviors associated with problem drinking? Explain how this type of drinking got its name.
   _____
   _____
   _____

2. What factors can affect a person's blood alcohol concentration?
   _____
   _____
   _____

3. Jane says that after drinking two cans of beer she feels she is a better, less timid driver. How does Jane's assessment of her driving ability after drinking two beers differ from her actual driving ability?
   _____
   _____
   _____

4. What indication might you have that a family member is becoming addicted to alcohol?
   _____
   _____

5. Your married sister thinks she may be pregnant. She has cut back on the amount she drinks and plans to stop drinking as soon as she confirms that she is pregnant. What advice might a physician give her?
   _____
   _____

6. Your father is taking sleeping pills that a physician prescribed for him. He wonders if it would be safe to have a cocktail before dinner. What might you tell him?
   _____
   _____

7. How can you avoid or refuse drinking alcohol in situations where other people are drinking?
   _____
   _____
   _____

Name _____ Date _____ Class _____

Personal Inventory
Smoking and Tobacco

Public opinion toward smokers and smoking is sharply divided. To look more closely at your own attitudes and behavior, complete these activities.

Finish these sentences with your opinions.

1. People who smoke _____
_____

2. The effects of smoking on the body are _____
_____

3. Banning smoking in public places is _____
_____

4. Warning labels on cigarette packs _____
_____

5. When someone near me lights a cigarette, _____
_____

Describe what you would do in each of these situations.

1. When I feel tense, upset, or uncomfortable,
   I usually _____

2. When I am bored or restless,
   I usually _____

3. When I am with people who are smoking,
   I usually _____

4. When I am asked to choose the smoking or nonsmoking section in a restaurant,
   I usually _____

5. When someone offers me a cigarette,
   I usually _____

6. When I am with someone who is trying to quit smoking,
   I usually _____

Look over your responses. Are you satisfied and comfortable with your behavior and attitudes toward smoking? _____ Are there any you would like to change? If so, which ones? _____

© Prentice-Hall, Inc.   Prentice Hall HEALTH: SKILLS FOR WELLNESS   77

Name _____ Date _____ Class _____

20 People and Tobacco
Practice

A number of factors influence a person's decision about whether or not to use tobacco. Most of these relate to health concerns and social pressures.

In the boxes below, write the social factors that influence a person's decision about tobacco use. In the circle, write the factor that greatly influences a person who chooses *not to use* tobacco, but that has little influence on a person who chooses *to use* tobacco. On the lines, write some of the undesirable effects of tobacco on a person who uses it.

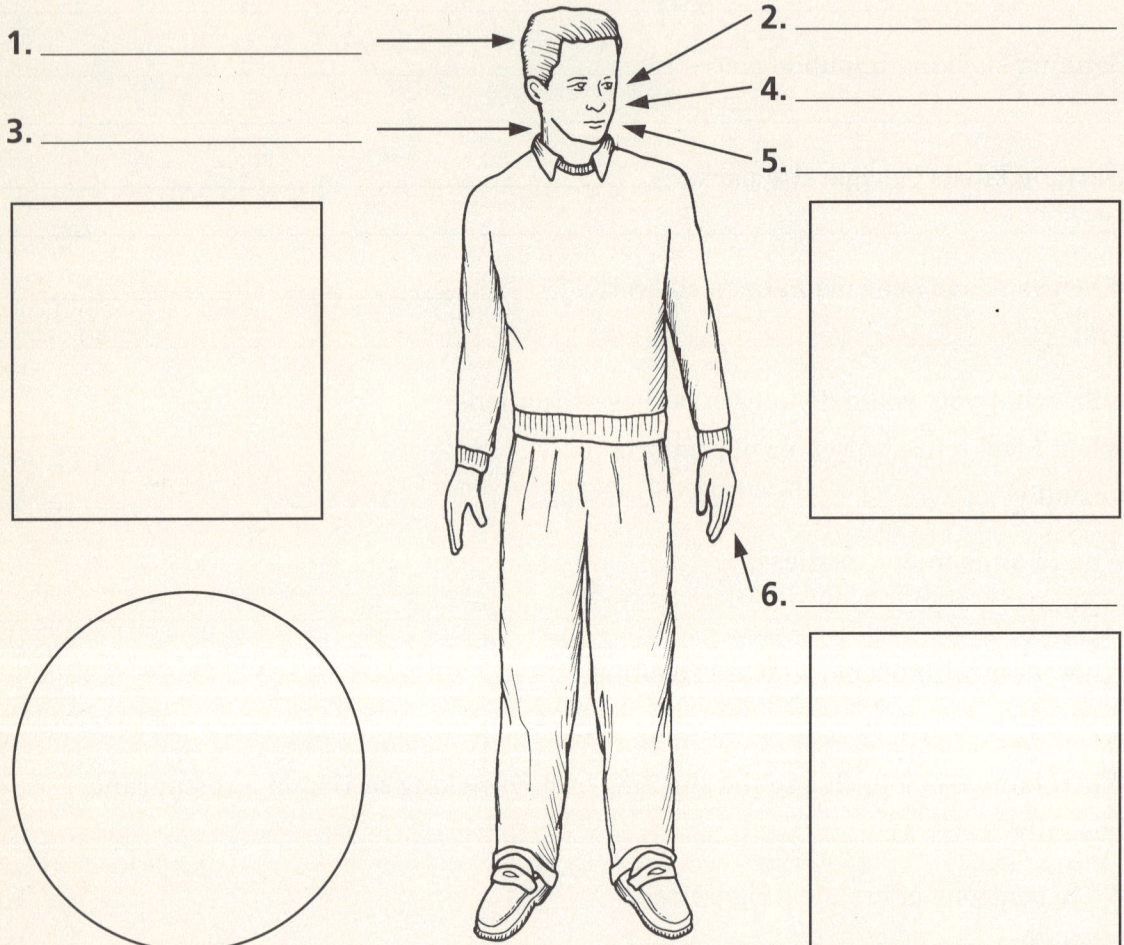

KEY
Boxes = social factors that influence a person's decision about tobacco use
Circle = factor that greatly influences a person who chooses *not to use* tobacco, but that has little influence on a person who chooses *to use* tobacco
Lines = undesirable effects of tobacco on a person who uses it

Prentice Hall HEALTH: SKILLS FOR WELLNESS   © Prentice-Hall, Inc.

Name _____ Date _____ Class _____

Chapter Review

Key Terms

Complete the following paragraphs using the list of words below. Each answer may be used once, more than once, or not at all.

carbon monoxide	snuff	nicotine withdrawal	chewing tobacco
chronic bronchitis	carcinogens	mainstream smoke	stimulant
tar	sidestream smoke	smokeless tobacco	oral cancers
leukoplakia	herbal cigarette	passive smokers	nicotine
emphysema	nicotine patch		

Tobacco is an addictive __(1)__ that speeds up the central nervous system, heart, and other organs. The drug in tobacco that causes these reactions is __(2)__. As with any addiction, when the smoker stops smoking, he or she suffers from __(3)__. The physical symptoms of this reaction include headache, irritability, and restlessness.

Tobacco contains other dangerous chemicals, many of which are __(4)__, or cancer-causing agents. The result of smoking is often lung cancer or __(5)__ of the mouth, throat, and tongue. These cancers often begin with __(6)__, which are hard, white, leathery patches in the mouth. These types of cancer are also the result of smoking tobacco products like pipe tobacco and cigars. Smokeless tobaccos include __(7)__, which is sniffed or held between the lower lip and teeth, and __(8)__, which is made of molasses or honey and tobacco leaves and is placed between the cheek and gums. Both are dangerous.

The dark, sticky mixture of chemicals that is produced when tobacco burns is called __(9)__. This mixture coats fingers and teeth, and it also coats lung passages and damages cilia. One of the gases produced in cigarette smoke is __(10)__, which reacts with the oxygen-carrying molecules in red blood cells and deprives the body of oxygen.

Tobacco also causes other health problems. One is __(11)__, a condition in which bronchial tubes become swollen and clogged with mucus. A more serious respiratory disease is __(12)__, in which the small air sacs in the lungs lose their ability to expand and contract.

The smoke that a smoker inhales and exhales is called __(13)__. The health of nonsmokers is threatened by __(14)__, which is the smoke that goes directly into the air when a cigarette burns. Just by breathing, nonsmokers become __(15)__, and they are at risk for the same health problems that smokers have.

1. _____
2. _____
3. _____
4. _____
5. _____
6. _____
7. _____
8. _____
9. _____
10. _____
11. _____
12. _____
13. _____
14. _____
15. _____

(Continued)

Name _____

Chapter Review (Continued)

Main Ideas

Answer each of the following questions.

1. Compare chronic bronchitis and emphysema. How are they alike? How are they different? _____
_____
_____
_____
_____
_____

2. What are three factors that influence people to start smoking? What are three factors that cause people to abstain from tobacco? _____
_____
_____
_____
_____
_____

Complete the chart below by supplying the information described in each column heading.

Substance	Chemicals It Contains	Physical Effects on the Body
3. Tobacco in cigarettes		
4. Smokeless tobacco		
5. Tobacco in cigars and pipes		
6. Passive smoke		

Name _____ Date _____ Class _____

Personal Inventory
Over-the-Counter Drugs

Advertising and widespread use have made over-the-counter drugs a part of everyday life. How much do you really know about these substances, which many people use so casually?

Each of the terms listed below describes a type of medicine that has a specific effect on the body. Next to each term, list this effect. If necessary, use a dictionary. Then write the name of an over-the-counter product that has this effect.

Type of Medicine	Effect on the Body	Product Name
Analgesic		
Antacid		
Antihistamine		
Antiseptic		
Astringent		
Decongestant		
Expectorant		

Finish these statements with your thoughts and feelings.

People use over-the-counter medicines to _____

_____

_____

Television and magazine ads for over-the-counter drugs are _____

_____

_____

Stores that sell over-the-counter drugs should _____

_____

_____

People who drive after taking a medicine that warns against driving because of its effects should _____

_____

_____

Taking over-the-counter medications with alcohol is _____

_____

_____

© Prentice-Hall, Inc.   Prentice Hall HEALTH: SKILLS FOR WELLNESS

Name _____ Date _____ Class _____

Practice
21 Risk Factors and Drug Abuse

Social factors, family factors, and personal factors all contribute to the risk of drug abuse among teenagers.

Working in small groups, describe a situation in which a teenager is at risk for drug abuse. Include one or more of the risk factors. Then role-play the situation. Afterwards, discuss what happened and suggest ways the teenager can prevent the risk of drug abuse. Role-play the situation again, incorporating the suggestions. Then discuss what happened the second time. Fill in the following form as you progress through the practice.

Situation: _____
_____
_____
_____
_____
_____

First role-play: _____
_____
_____
_____
_____
_____

What a teenager can do to prevent risk of drug abuse: _____
_____
_____
_____
_____
_____

Second role-play: _____
_____
_____
_____
_____
_____

Prentice Hall HEALTH: SKILLS FOR WELLNESS © Prentice-Hall, Inc.

Name _____ Date _____ Class _____

Chapter Review

Key Terms

Match each word with its correct definition. Some words may not be used.

narcotics	cocaine	psychoactive drugs
look-alike drugs	side effects	stimulant
prescription drug	amphetamines	detoxification program
synergistic interaction	anabolic steroids	designer drug
methadone	inhalants	tranquilizer

1. drugs abused by athletes to build bigger bodies
2. drugs that are absorbed through the lungs
3. chemicals that affect the activity of brain cells to alter perception, mood, and thought
4. highly addictive stimulant that causes depression when its effect wears off
5. depressant drugs made from or similar to opium
6. new chemical substance that has been designed to be similar to a controlled substance
7. treatment involving gradual but complete withdrawal from the abused drug
8. drug used to treat heroin dependence
9. unwanted physical and mental reactions to a drug
10. commonly abused anti-anxiety drug
11. drugs made to look like commonly abused drugs; can contain any kind of substance
12. drug interaction in which the action of a drug is increased

1. _____
2. _____
3. _____
4. _____
5. _____
6. _____
7. _____
8. _____
9. _____
10. _____
11. _____
12. _____

Complete the following paragraph using the list of words below. Each answer may be used once, more than once, or not at all.

| side effects | depressant | action |
| overdose | antagonistic | |

The __(13)__ of a drug often varies in different people. A physician determines the correct amount for an individual at the time a prescription is written. Unfortunately, many drugs have __(14)__ that may be undesirable. A person may think that taking a larger dose of a prescribed drug will speed recovery, but an excessive amount of a drug can produce a serious, even fatal, reaction called a(n) __(15)__. When two drugs are taken at the same time, the effect of one may cancel the effect of the other, producing a(n) __(16)__ effect.

13. _____
14. _____
15. _____
16. _____

(Continued)

© Prentice-Hall, Inc.   Prentice Hall HEALTH: SKILLS FOR WELLNESS   83

Name _____

Chapter Review (Continued)

Main Ideas
Answer each of the following questions in two or three sentences.

1. Name the three major types of risk factors for drug abuse among teenagers. _____
_____
_____
_____

2. Suppose a psychoactive drug abuser does not experience physical withdrawal symptoms after not taking the drug for a short period of time. Does that mean the person is not addicted to the drug? Explain. _____
_____
_____
_____
_____

3. Explain the difference between the three types of drug treatment centers.
_____
_____
_____

Complete the chart below by supplying the information described in each column heading.

Category of Drug	Examples of Drug	Effects on Body
4. Depressants		
5. Stimulants		
6. Hallucinogens		

Name _____ Date _____ Class _____

Personal Inventory
Immunization Record

Use this chart to make and keep an accurate record of your childhood infectious diseases and the immunizations you have received. This information can come from your parents, your physicians, or written records you may have from school or camp.

My Record of Immunizations

Vaccine	Original (month/year)	Booster (month/year)		Physician/Clinic
Diphtheria-tetanus-pertussis		1		
		2		
		3		
		4		
Polio		1		
		2		
		3		
Hepatitis B		1		
		2		
Measles-mumps-rubella				
Haemophilus influenzae type b		1		
		2		
		3		
Varicella zoster (chicken pox)				

My Record of Childhood Infectious Diseases

Measles _____
Mumps _____
Chicken pox _____
Rubella _____

Whooping cough _____
(pertussis)
Pneumonia _____
Other _____

Name _____ Date _____ Class _____

22 Defending Against Infection

Practice

The body uses three lines of defense to guard against infection: physical and chemical defense systems, inflammation, and the immune system.

Identify the line of defense used in the infectious situations listed in the left column of the chart below. Then fill in the right column of the chart using your own words. A sample is provided.

Use the following code system to save space: P & C = physical and chemical defense systems; INF = inflammation; IMM = immune system.

Infectious Situation	Body's Line of Defense
Bacteria and pathogens on skin surface	P & C—hard skin cells with no gaps keep out pathogens; sweat acids kill bacteria; pathogens shed with old skin
Pathogens in nose, mouth, or eyes	
Pathogens in digestive tract	
Pathogens in burn or cut	
Influenza virus enters body for first time	
Chicken-pox virus enters body for second time	
Measles virus enters body soon after measles vaccination	
Rabies pathogens enter body from bite by rabid dog	

Name _____ Date _____ Class _____

Chapter Review

Key Terms

Use the clues to identify the words. Write each word on the line following the clue. Then find and circle each word in the word search puzzle below.

1. organism that causes disease
2. simple, single-celled microorganisms that can live almost anywhere
3. proteins that attach to the surface of pathogens
4. body's ability to destroy pathogens that it has previously encountered, thereby preventing disease
5. a regulatory substance that T cells produce
6. disease that can cause birth defects when pregnant women contract it in the first few months of pregnancy
7. drug that inhibits or kills bacteria
8. injected substance that contains small amounts of dead or modified pathogens or their toxins

1. _____
2. _____
3. _____
4. _____
5. _____
6. _____
7. _____
8. _____

```
B I T N A O H N I T N A
V M H O P A T H O G E N
A M I R E A U L N D A S
N U F E L I L S T I N R
T N R U B E L L A J T U
I I C V A C C I N E I F
B T C O C N A M M U B E
O Y I D T E W U S T I H
D U L A E R F T G O O N
I N T E R F E R O N T A
E E H N I B O D W M I C
S P A T A E R S S N C F
```

Define or describe the following terms.

9. incubation stage _____

10. infectious diseases _____

11. lymphocytes _____

(Continued)

Name _____

Chapter Review (Continued)

Main Ideas

Answer each of the following questions.

1. What is the difference between the ways bacteria and viruses injure body cells? _____
_____
_____

2. In what ways does the digestive tract act as a barrier to pathogens? _____
_____
_____

Complete the chart below.

Infectious Disease	Pathogen	How Spread	Symptoms
3.			sneezing, sore throat, coughing, runny nose, chest congestion, fever, headache, muscle aches
4.			fatigue, weight loss, mild fever, night sweats, chronic cough
5. Influenza			
6.		transmitted in human wastes, contaminated water, and contaminated food, especially shellfish	

88   Prentice Hall HEALTH: SKILLS FOR WELLNESS   © Prentice-Hall, Inc.

Name _____ Date _____ Class _____

23 Thoughts About AIDS and STDs

Personal Inventory

It is difficult for most people to think clearly and honestly about emotional issues such as AIDS and other sexually transmitted diseases (STDs). To understand your feelings, list the words you think of when you hear the terms *AIDS* and *STDs*.

Write quickly. Try not to censor your thoughts. Do not worry about spelling or neatness. Stop after five minutes.

Acquired Immunodeficiency Syndrome (AIDS)

_____ _____ _____
_____ _____ _____
_____ _____ _____

Sexually Transmitted Diseases (STDs)

_____ _____ _____
_____ _____ _____
_____ _____ _____

Review your lists. What kinds of feelings do you associate with these terms?
_____
_____
_____

What did you discover about your feelings about AIDS? _____
_____
_____
_____

What were your feelings about other STDs? _____
_____
_____
_____

Were there any inaccurate or irrelevant words included in your lists? Which words? Why do you think you included them? _____
_____
_____
_____

© Prentice-Hall, Inc. Prentice Hall HEALTH: SKILLS FOR WELLNESS

Name _____ Date _____ Class _____

Practice
The Silent Epidemic

Knowing the facts about sexually transmitted diseases (STDs) is an important part of the battle against the silent epidemic of STDs.

First, fill in the definitions. Then, in the outline below, fill in the facts about STDs. Choose one of the facts to put on a poster.

Definition of sexually transmitted diseases (STDs): _____
_____

Definition of epidemic: _____
_____

   I. Reasons for concern about STDs
      A. _____
      B. _____
      C. _____
      D. _____
      E. _____

  II. Reasons for the STDs epidemic
      A. _____
      B. _____
      C. _____

III. How to avoid STDs
      A. _____
      B. _____
      C. _____
      D. _____

IV. Healthy choices
      A. _____
      B. _____
      C. _____
      D. Measures to prevent further spread
          1. _____
          2. _____
          3. _____
          4. _____

Chapter Review

Key Terms

Complete the following paragraphs using the list of words below. Each word may be used once, more than once, or not at all.

acquired immuno-
   deficiency syndrome
chancroid
candidiasis
genital herpes
pneumocystis carinii
   pneumonia

pelvic inflammatory
   disease
human papilloma
   virus
congenital syphilis
pubic lice

human immuno-
   deficiency virus
sexual fidelity
scabies
trichomoniasis
hepatitis B

opportunistic
   diseases
genital warts
chlamydia
sexual abstinence
syphilis

Sexually transmitted diseases (STDs) can be very painful and, if left untreated, can result in permanent body damage, and sometimes death. Fortunately STDs are largely preventable. Because STDs are spread primarily by sexual intercourse, the most certain way to avoid STDs is to practice __(1)__. For two uninfected people who are involved in a sexual relationship, the most certain way to avoid STDs is to have sexual intercourse only with one another—in other words, to practice __(2)__.

Although a few STDs are characterized by a lack of symptoms, most have distinct symptoms that can lead to early diagnosis and treatment. Early diagnosis and treatment is especially important for __(3)__, a serious bacterial STD that progresses through several distinct stages but is only curable in its early stages. (In the early stages, this STD resembles another STD, __(4)__, which is characterized by deep, painful sores around the genitals.) At any stage of the disease, a pregnant woman can pass the disease to her developing baby. The baby will be born with __(5)__, which damages the baby's skin, bones, eyes, teeth, and liver.

The most common bacterial STD in the United States is __(6)__. If untreated in females, this disease can result in a serious infection of the reproductive organs called __(7)__.

The most common viral STD in the United States is __(8)__. Once a person is infected, the virus remains in the body for life. Another incurable viral STD is __(9)__, which produces painful blisters around the genitals. __(10)__ is a sexually transmitted disease that attacks the liver. Since the virus that causes this disease can also be spread by blood-to-blood contact, it is important that infected persons not share toothbrushes, razors, or eating utensils with other people.

Two conditions involving infestation of tiny animal parasites can be sexually transmitted: __(11)__ and __(12)__, which result from an infestation of mites.

1. _____
2. _____
3. _____
4. _____
5. _____
6. _____
7. _____
8. _____
9. _____
10. _____
11. _____
12. _____
13. _____
14. _____
15. _____

(Continued)

Name _____

Chapter Review (Continued)

__(13)__ is the pathogen that causes an STD that weakens the body's immune system by attacking certain T cells. The last and most severe stage of this disease is __(14)__, which is characterized by the appearance of __(15)__, such as tuberculosis and Kaposi's sarcoma.

Main Ideas
Answer each of the following questions.

1. Describe the similarities between chlamydia and gonorrhea. _____
_____
_____

2. What are four ways of avoiding or greatly reducing the risk of getting a sexually transmitted disease? _____
_____
_____
_____

3. What kinds of treatments are available to people with HIV infection and AIDS? Explain your answer. _____
_____
_____
_____

4. Saleem has been practicing behaviors that place him at risk for HIV infection. He notices that his glands are swollen, he is always tired, and he has been losing a lot of weight during the past six months. He strongly suspects he has AIDS, but he prefers not to find out and wants to carry on his life in a "business-as-usual" manner. How can you convince him to see a physician and be tested? _____
_____
_____
_____

5. Why should people engaging in high-risk behavior be tested frequently for the presence of HIV antibodies in the blood? _____
_____
_____
_____

Name _____ Date _____ Class _____

Personal Inventory
Family Health History

Use this chart to obtain a health history of your family or another family you know. In the column headed "Family Member," write the name of any close relative who has or had this disease or disorder. ("Close relatives" include a person's parents, grandparents, and brothers and sisters, as well as brothers and sisters of the person's parents and grandparents.) If the disease caused a death, include the date of death. Good sources of information include family records or a knowledgeable older relative.

Condition	Family Member	Condition	Family Member
Alcoholism		Liver disease	
Allergies		Migraine headache	
Anemia		Obesity	
Arthritis		Osteoporosis	
Asthma/Hay fever		Rheumatic fever	
Blood disorders		Sickle-cell disease	
Cancer		Stroke	
Diabetes		Thyroid disorder	
Emphysema		Tuberculosis	
Epilepsy		Ulcers	
Hearing disorders		Visual problems	
Heart disease		Birth defects	
High blood pressure		Inherited genetic disorders	
Kidney disease		Other health problems	

What did you learn about the family that you did not know before? _____
_____
_____

What could family members do to reduce their risk for each of the conditions that appear in their family health history? _____
_____
_____

© Prentice-Hall, Inc.   Prentice Hall HEALTH: SKILLS FOR WELLNESS   93

Name _____ Date _____ Class _____

24 Understanding Disabilities
Practice

You may know someone who has a physical disability. Understanding disabilities can help you interact with that person in a positive manner.

One way to better understand a disability is to participate in a simulation exercise. In a simulation exercise, you can experience something similar to what a person with a disability experiences.

Your teacher will arrange for a simulation of one or more physical disabilities. After you have completed the simulation exercise, discuss the following questions:

1. How did you feel during the simulation exercise? _____
_____
_____

2. What are the three most common disabilities? _____
_____
_____

3. Which disabilities were simulated in the exercise? _____
_____
_____

4. Do you think the exercise simulated a slight, moderate, or severe degree of impairment? Explain your answer. _____
_____
_____

5. What may cause disabilities such as those you experienced in the simulation exercise?
_____
_____
_____

6. What devices or techniques could people with such disabilities use to help themselves?
_____
_____
_____

7. How would you want people to treat you if you had disabilities such as those you experienced in the simulation exercise? _____
_____
_____

94 Prentice Hall HEALTH: SKILLS FOR WELLNESS

Chapter Review

Key Terms

On the line at the right, write the letter of the word or phrase that matches each numbered description below. Each answer may be used once, more than once, or not at all.

- **a.** oncogenes
- **b.** biopsy
- **c.** cholesterol
- **d.** fibrillation
- **e.** diabetes
- **f.** electrocardiogram
- **g.** atherosclerosis
- **h.** disability
- **i.** arrhythmia
- **j.** metastasis
- **k.** aneurysm

1. life-threatening type of irregular heartbeat in which the heart twitches in an uncoordinated way
2. disease in which fatlike substances are deposited inside artery walls
3. blood-filled weak spot ballooning out from the artery wall
4. irregular heartbeats
5. recording of the heart's electrical activity
6. spread of cancer from the place it develops to other parts of the body
7. genes that cause cancer when exposed to carcinogens
8. microscopic examination of a small piece of tissue for signs of cancer
9. physical or mental impairment that limits or reduces normal activities
10. disease in which the ability of the body to use blood sugar is impaired

1. _____
2. _____
3. _____
4. _____
5. _____
6. _____
7. _____
8. _____
9. _____
10. _____

Complete the following paragraphs using the list of words below. Each answer may be used once, more than once, or not at all.

cerebral hemorrhage	coronary bypass	cardiopulmonary	leukemia
artificial pacemaker	high blood pressure	resuscitation	cardiovascular
rheumatic heart	fibrillation	coronary heart	plaque

The most common type of noninfectious disease in the United States is __(11)__ disease. The "silent killer," or __(12)__, is a form of this disease.

Blockage of the arteries that supply blood to the heart muscle is __(13)__ disease. Treatment of this condition may include __(14)__ surgery.

In cases of stroke, blood flow to a part of the brain is suddenly disrupted. Sometimes an artery in the main part of the brain bursts, resulting in a(n) __(15)__.

One heart valve disease is __(16)__ disease, which results from rheumatic fever caused by the same bacteria that cause strep throat. Abnormal heartbeat can be controlled by a(n) __(17)__.

11. _____
12. _____
13. _____
14. _____
15. _____
16. _____
17. _____

(Continued)

Name _____

Chapter Review (Continued)

Main Ideas
Answer each of the following questions.

1. In what way is congestive heart failure related to high blood pressure? _____
_____
_____
_____

2. How is a heart attack different from a stroke? _____
_____
_____
_____

Complete the following chart by supplying the information described in each column heading.

Type of Cancer	Classification (Hereditary, Environmental, Behavioral) and Cause	Symptoms	Prevention
3.			To protect against the sun's ultraviolet rays, wear protective clothing, sunglasses, and use sunscreen
4.		Difficult to detect in early stage; persistent cough, chest pain, repeated attacks of pneumonia or bronchitis	
5. Oral (lips, tongue, mouth, throat)	Behavioral; caused by tobacco use of any kind; linked to excessive alcohol use		
6.	Behavioral; diet high in fat and low in fiber		Eat high-fiber foods; trim fat from diet

Name _____ Date _____ Class _____

Personal Inventory
You and the Environment

People and businesses who are planning projects that might affect water, land, air, or wildlife are often required to make reports called Environmental Impact Statements. If you had to make such a report based on your behavior, what would it show?

For each of the situations below, circle the letter of the answer that describes what you would do. Then, in the right-hand column, describe what you think would be the environmental impact if many people chose the same behavior.

Situation	Environmental Impact

1. When you need to go to a nearby store, what do you do?
   a. Drive or get a ride.
   b. Walk or ride a bicycle.
   c. Use public transportation.	

2. What do you do with used paint thinner?
   a. Store it in a safe place.
   b. Ask the local health department what to do.
   c. Pour it down the drain.	

3. When your sidewalks are icy, what do you do?
   a. Throw sand on them.
   b. Spread salt on them.
   c. Leave them as they are.	

4. When you rake leaves, what do you do?
   a. Burn them.
   b. Put them in a compost pile.
   c. Throw them away in plastic or paper bags.	

5. How do you choose among similar products?
   a. Buy those in biodegradable packages.
   b. Buy those in plastic wrap.
   c. Do not think about the packaging.	

6. When buying products in spray cans, what do you do?
   a. Buy the same brand every time.
   b. Choose an aerosol can.
   c. Look for products with pump tops.	

7. What do you do with fast-food containers?
   a. Toss the used boxes and cans out of the car window.
   b. Find a trash can for the litter.
   c. Put all the trash in a bag in the car.	

Which of your behaviors might you think about changing? Why? _____
_____

© Prentice-Hall, Inc.   Prentice Hall HEALTH: SKILLS FOR WELLNESS

Name _____ Date _____ Class _____

Practice
Warning Signs

The effects of radiation and noise pollution pose serious threats to your health.

With a partner, discuss the sources and effects of these health threats and the preventive measures that can be taken against them. Write your answers to the following questions during your discussions.

1. What are some of the normal sources of radiation exposure for most people?
   _____
   _____
   _____

2. What are the dangers of high-level radiation exposure from these normal sources?
   _____
   _____
   _____

3. What kind of preventive measures can people take against high-level radiation from these normal sources? _____
   _____
   _____

4. What are some other sources of high-level radiation? _____
   _____
   _____

5. In what way can loud music be considered a threat to your health? _____
   _____
   _____
   _____

6. Summarize the recent breakthrough that could prevent the risk of high-level radiation exposure from water contaminated by radioactive uranium. _____
   _____
   _____
   _____

Prentice Hall HEALTH: SKILLS FOR WELLNESS

Name _____ Date _____ Class _____

Chapter Review

Key Terms
Use the clues to identify the terms. Then find the terms in the word-search puzzle on the next page.

1. the use over and over again of materials such as metal and glass
2. formed when nitrogen oxide gas mixes with water
3. produced when water combines with sulfur oxide and/or nitrogen oxide
4. formed when hydrocarbons react with nitric oxide in the presence of sunlight
5. region of the atmosphere that absorbs ultraviolet rays from the sun
6. disease that results when a person inhales asbestos fibers
7. waste material carried from toilets and drains
8. chemicals that kill weeds
9. small water plants
10. process of excessive algae growth followed by decay and lack of oxygen
11. materials that are flammable, explosive, corrosive, or toxic to humans
12. cancer-causing substances
13. loud sound that is a nuisance or can harm your health if present over a certain level
14. radioactive gas linked to lung cancer
15. radioactivity that falls to the ground in rain or snow
16. area where trash, garbage, and other wastes are deposited and covered with soil
17. accumulation of harmful wastes or other harmful substances in the environment
18. unit for measuring the loudness of sound

1. _____
2. _____
3. _____
4. _____
5. _____
6. _____
7. _____
8. _____
9. _____
10. _____
11. _____
12. _____
13. _____
14. _____
15. _____
16. _____
17. _____
18. _____

(Continued)

Chapter Review (Continued)

```
L V E U T R O P H I C A T I O N
A C W N E D C Q A O F N I S H O
N A R I W B J D Z C S M O G E I
D R X T F H H O A B I R M S R S
F C Q R A F N W R X J D O E B E
I I R I L E R A D O N E R W I P
L N E C L Z N L O R V C W A C S
L O C A O T N G U F V I W G I N
E G Y C U G N A S X K B T E D N
F E C I T U W E W B M E A Z E Y
R N L D B I D S A W C L T M S P
R S I G A S B E S T O S I S X N
A E N P O L L U T I O N I O U F
V S G W T I U I E C B S E R S N
```

Main Ideas

Answer each of the following questions.

1. There is an oil spill in the North Sea off the coast of Scotland. An environmentalist says the spill shows us why we should use electric cars. Why does she say that?
   _____
   _____

2. Compare and contrast carbon monoxide and carbon dioxide. _____
   _____
   _____

3. A scientist says chlorofluorocarbons may lead to an increase in skin cancer. Explain.
   _____
   _____

4. In what ways can you help to conserve water each day? _____
   _____
   _____

5. Why are bacteria and other microorganisms no longer an effective means of breaking down biodegradable wastes? _____
   _____

6. Why should landfills be sealed? _____
   _____

Prentice Hall HEALTH: SKILLS FOR WELLNESS © Prentice-Hall, Inc.

Name _____ Date _____ Class _____

Personal Inventory
Health-Care Choices

Just as consumers make choices among sweaters, cars, records, and other things they buy, consumers also need to make choices when they buy health care. To discover what some of these choices are—and what you need to know to make them wisely—consider what you would do in each of these situations.

In some cases, several choices may be good ones. Put a check beside any you choose. Then give the reasons for your decision.

1. If I were buying health insurance, I would choose

   _____ a thorough group plan in which I picked my own physician.
   _____ a simple, inexpensive plan covering hospitalization only.
   _____ a health maintenance organization with its own staff.

Reasons: _____
_____

2. If I strained a muscle playing sports, I would

   _____ go to a hospital or clinic emergency room.
   _____ call a physician.
   _____ use ice and an elastic bandage at home.

Reasons: _____
_____

3. If I were told I had a serious illness, I would want to

   _____ do whatever my physician advised.
   _____ ask to have a second opinion from another physician.
   _____ look for a clinic offering a new "miracle" treatment.

Reasons: _____
_____

4. If I moved to a new town and needed to find a physician, I would

   _____ look in the phone book for someone with an office nearby.
   _____ consider only female (or only male) physicians.
   _____ ask my former physicians for recommendations.

Reasons: _____
_____

© Prentice-Hall, Inc.   Prentice Hall HEALTH: SKILLS FOR WELLNESS

Name _____ Date _____ Class _____

Practice
Paying for Health Care

Most people do not have enough money to pay for all of their health care, so they choose a health-care insurance plan that pays for a major part of their medical expenses.

Fill out the chart below to understand better the types of health insurance plans available. Write a brief summary of the advantages and disadvantages of each plan.

	HEALTH INSURANCE PLANS		
	Conventional Health Insurance	**Managed-Care Health Insurance**	**Government-Supported Health Insurance**
Eligible People			
Cost			
Type of Health Care Covered			
Choice of Health-Care Services			

102   Prentice Hall HEALTH: SKILLS FOR WELLNESS   © Prentice-Hall, Inc.

Name _____ Date _____ Class _____

Chapter Review

Key Terms

Complete the following crossword puzzle.

Across

4. an unpleasant response of your body to medicine
6. short-term facility that focuses on helping a dying patient live as comfortably as possible
8. the amount of medical expense that the individual must pay
9. federally funded insurance program for elderly people

Down

1. facility where primary health care is provided by one or more physicians
2. standard name of a prescription drug
3. branch of medicine that emphasizes the relationship of the body's muscular and skeletal systems to general health
5. anyone who buys goods and services
7. group of physicians and other health-care workers that provides complete medical services to its members

Define or describe the following terms.

10. secondary health care _____

11. convalescent home _____

12. managed care _____

(Continued)

Name _____

Chapter Review (Continued)

Main Ideas
Answer each of the following questions.

1. How is seeing a physician in a clinic different from seeing your own physician in his or her office? _____
_____
_____

2. What could you do if you felt uneasy about a treatment recommended by your physician? _____
_____
_____

3. How could you have a large medical bill even if you are covered by group insurance? _____
_____
_____

4. How can quackery be dangerous? _____
_____
_____

5. What is the difference between a nurse and a nurse practitioner? _____
_____
_____

6. Distinguish between a specialty hospital and a teaching hospital. _____
_____
_____

7. How does a convalescent home differ from a nursing home? _____
_____
_____

Name _____ Date _____ Class _____

Personal Inventory
Public Health Concerns

Issues concerning public health are frequently in the news. Some current major public health concerns are listed below. How important are they to *you*? Use a rating scale of 1 to 10 to show your concern about each issue listed. The issue that most concerns you should rank number 1 in your rating.

_____ Child abuse

_____ Purity and safety of foods

_____ AIDS research

_____ Substance abuse

_____ Homeless persons

_____ Famine and world hunger

_____ Mandatory drug testing by employers

_____ Air and water pollution

_____ Toxic and nuclear waste disposal

_____ Nuclear disarmament

What issues would you add to this list? _____

_____

Would you delete any issues? Which ones? _____

_____

_____

Were you surprised at the ratings you gave certain issues? Why? _____

_____

_____

_____

What thoughts and feelings did you have as you read the issues on this list? _____

_____

_____

_____

What did you learn from this exercise about things that matter to you? _____

_____

_____

_____

© Prentice-Hall, Inc.   Prentice Hall HEALTH: SKILLS FOR WELLNESS

Name _____ Date _____ Class _____

27 International Public Health

Practice

International organizations work with people in developing nations throughout the world to help them overcome a great variety of health problems. These problems result from a lack of basic necessities like food, water, and shelter.

International public health organizations have different sponsors. In the chart below, list those organizations that are sponsored by the United Nations, the United States government, and by private sponsors. Include in your list the main services of five of these organizations. Then choose one of the organizations and make a classroom poster illustrating its services.

United Nations	U.S. Government	Private Sponsors

Name _____ Date _____ Class _____

Chapter Review

Key Terms
Complete the following paragraphs using the list of words and phrases below. Each word or phrase may be used once, more than once, or not at all.

famine	epidemiology	vital statistics	Public Health Service
quarantine	statistics	public health	Health and Human Services
health codes	high-risk populations	cholera	

All the government agencies and private organizations that work to prevent disease and promote positive health behaviors make up the __(1)__ system. For centuries the only ways to combat epidemics were through disinfection or through __(2)__, which is a period of isolation imposed on people who have been exposed to an infectious disease. One such disease was __(3)__, an infectious disease of the small intestine. In 1850, Dr. John Snow studied this disease in an area of London and learned how it was transmitted—through bacteria-contaminated water. This sort of study is an example of __(4)__. The goal is to identify dangerous health practices in __(5)__, those people who are most likely to get a certain disease.

1. _____
2. _____
3. _____
4. _____
5. _____
6. _____
7. _____
8. _____
9. _____

Most public health activities are carried out by state and local governments. An important function of local health offices is the recording of __(6)__, which provide the number of births, deaths, and the numbers and kinds of diseases within a population. Local health departments also enforce state __(7)__, which are standards for factors that affect health, such as water quality.

At the federal level, the Department of __(8)__ has the widest range of responsibilities for public health. One of the divisions within this agency is the __(9)__, which is made up of several departments, each with its own programs and functions.

Define or describe the following terms.

10. Centers for Disease Control and Prevention _____
_____

11. National Institutes of Health _____
_____

12. Health Resources and Services Administration _____
_____

13. oral-rehydration therapy _____
_____

14. International Committee of the Red Cross _____
_____

(Continued)

Name _____

Chapter Review (Continued)

Main Ideas
Complete the chart below.

Public Health Service	Function
1. Food and Drug Administration	
2.	provides comprehensive health care for Native Americans
3. Agency for Toxic Substances and Disease Registry	
4.	protects the public from environmental hazards; enforces laws that regulate pollution

Answer each of the following questions.

5. What are the specific tasks of a public health system in today's world?
_____
_____
_____

6. Why are private health services needed?
_____
_____
_____

7. What are five functions of state government health agencies?
_____
_____
_____

Name _____ Date _____ Class _____

Personal Inventory
Safety Risks

Most unintentional injuries happen at home. For teenagers, however, motor vehicles and bikes can also be risky. How careful are you on the street? In and around your home? How often do you think about reducing the risk of unintentional injuries?

Read each item below. Put a check in the column that describes your behavior.

Reducing Risk	Always	Usually	Sometimes	Seldom/ Never
1. I wear a safety belt when I ride in a motor vehicle.				
2. I ride my bicycle only in daylight.				
3. I wear a helmet when I ride my bike.				
4. I watch for motor vehicle doors opening when I am riding my bike on city streets.				
5. I avoid riding with friends who have bad driving records.				
6. I am careful when using and storing flammable fluids.				
7. I put poisonous substances in places where small children cannot reach them.				
8. I avoid touching electrical appliances with wet hands or when standing near water.				
9. I unplug appliances when they are not in use.				
10. Before mowing a lawn, I check for rocks and sticks.				
11. I wear shoes when mowing a lawn.				
12. I avoid piling things on steps or stairways.				
13. I turn on a light when looking for something at night.				
14. I avoid swimming alone.				

© Prentice-Hall, Inc.   Prentice Hall HEALTH: SKILLS FOR WELLNESS

Name _____ Date _____ Class _____

Practice
Avoiding Violence

Protecting yourself against violence is part of staying healthy. Various situations may lead to violence.

On the lines provided, suggest what you should do in each situation below to protect yourself against assault. Then create a poster that tells how to avoid violence in a dangerous situation.

A. Your car has broken down on a busy highway. _____
_____
_____
_____
_____
_____

B. You are home alone. A stranger knocks at your door asking for help. _____
_____
_____
_____
_____
_____

C. You are returning to your car in a parking lot. _____
_____
_____
_____
_____
_____

D. You are being followed by a stranger as you walk down a deserted street at night.
_____
_____
_____
_____
_____
_____

Name _____ Date _____ Class _____

Chapter Review

Key Terms
Use the clues to identify the terms. Then find the terms in the word-search puzzle below.

1. action that increases a person's chances of a harmful outcome
2. heavy snowstorm with winds over 34 miles per hour
3. sudden, catastrophic event affecting many people
4. government agency that identifies occupational hazards and sets standards for safety
5. rapidly rotating column of air
6. results when a person's air supply is cut off
7. unlawful attempt or threat to harm someone

1. _____
2. _____
3. _____
4. _____
5. _____
6. _____
7. _____

```
C A H K O S H L E F M G
R S H B L I Z Z A R D E
O A L I A B O E F A C T
I C A S L I D D R K N O
V C S I C L A F W O N R
A I S U A I N I I O E N
H D A E P T R T W T A A
E E U L S A A A S A C D
B N L S I C T A N T I O
K T T E O O S I R I C D
S A N F E I D I O S H A
I A F A D A M S T N Z K
R U S H A P I W T A A I
S M N T A U C C O L B L
```

Define or describe the following terms.

8. flammable material _____
_____

9. Poison Control Center _____
_____

(Continued)

Name _____

Chapter Review (Continued)

10. electrocution _____
_____

11. Operation Identification _____
_____

Main Ideas
Answer each of the following questions.

1. What are four factors that you should keep in mind to help you reduce the risk of unintentional injuries? _____
_____
_____

2. What can be done to make a workplace safer? _____
_____
_____

3. What are common causes of capsizing in small boats? _____
_____
_____

4. What are three ways to avoid sports injuries? _____
_____
_____

5. People of which age group have the highest rate of motor-vehicle crashes? _____
_____
_____

6. What should you do if your car breaks down far from help? _____
_____
_____

7. What is the relationship between alcohol consumption and motor-vehicle crashes?
_____
_____

8. What is one way you can help to reduce crime? _____
_____
_____

Name _____ Date _____ Class _____

Personal Inventory

29 Observing and Interpreting Warning Signs

How much help you can be in an emergency situation often depends on your ability to observe and interpret warning signs.

1. In order to be able to provide the quick response that is important in so many life-threatening situations, you need to be able to anticipate problems. What things that you see, smell, or hear might alert you to the fact that someone nearby needs help?

   _____
   _____
   _____
   _____
   _____

2. Someone who needs first aid may not be able to tell you what's wrong. It may be up to you to infer what happened by observing the person's condition and surroundings. What warning signs do you know for each of the following?

   a. stroke _____
   _____
   _____

   b. head injury _____
   _____
   _____

   c. snakebite _____
   _____
   _____

   d. allergic reaction to insect sting _____
   _____
   _____

   e. shock _____
   _____
   _____

© Prentice-Hall, Inc.　　Prentice Hall HEALTH: SKILLS FOR WELLNESS

Name _____ Date _____ Class _____

29 Responding to Emergencies

Practice

Those who spend time outdoors may encounter situations in which they are exposed to health risks. It is important to know how to handle outdoor health emergencies.

With a partner, make flash cards for each of the following outdoor emergencies: snakebite, insect sting, animal bite, drowning, frostbite, hypothermia, heat exhaustion, and heatstroke. On one side of the card, write the signs indicating the emergency situation. On the other side, identify the emergency. Take turns choosing cards, reading the signs, and then identifying the emergencies based on the signs.

Then, with your partner, dramatize four situations, each involving one of these outdoor emergencies. In each dramatization, one person should be the individual at risk, acting out the signs that indicate the emergency situation. The other person should act out the appropriate response procedures. Afterward, discuss what happened in each situation and fill in the following chart.

Emergency Situation	How You Handled the Situation

114 Prentice Hall HEALTH: SKILLS FOR WELLNESS © Prentice-Hall, Inc.

Name _____ Date _____ Class _____

 **Chapter Review**

Key Terms
Complete the following crossword puzzle.

Across
1. a separation of the bone from its joint
4. rapid, deep breathing that lowers the carbon dioxide level in the blood
6. freezing of body tissue caused by long exposure to cold
7. condition that occurs when a blood vessel in the brain breaks or a blood clot forms and blocks blood flow to the brain
9. rigid material tied to an injured part of the body to keep it from moving

Down
2. alternating periods of severe muscular contraction and relaxation
3. temporary loss of consciousness
4. severe bleeding that can result in shock and death if not properly treated
5. condition in which the heart fails to adequately circulate blood to vital organs
8. potentially fatal bacterial disease that can be transmitted by an animal bite

Supply the correct term that fits each of the following descriptions.

10. break or crack in a bone in which the broken bone does not push through the skin surface _____

11. law that protects people from lawsuits if medical complications arise after they have administered first aid correctly _____

12. a serious loss of body heat that causes the body temperature to fall well below normal _____

(Continued)

© Prentice-Hall, Inc.   Prentice Hall HEALTH: SKILLS FOR WELLNESS   115

Name _____

Chapter Review (Continued)

Main Ideas
Complete the following chart.

Type of Emergency	First-Aid Procedure
1. Cardiac arrest	
2. Severe bleeding	
3.	Call Poison Control Center immediately. If victim is unconscious, use rescue breathing through nose. Get help.
4. Sprain	
5. Electrical shock	

Answer each of the following questions in two or three sentences.

6. What conditions should be cared for first in an emergency? _____
_____
_____
_____
_____

7. What do you need to do if you are the first person at the scene of an injury? _____
_____
_____
_____
_____